Contents

Wild Winds

They watched it explode into the air on March 18, 1925. It set records at a speed of 73 miles per hour and a path length of 219 miles. Three and one-half hours later, 695 people had died and 2,027 were injured. The damage covered three states—Missouri, Illinois, and Indiana. It became known as the Tri-State Tornado.

It's hard to believe that one tornado could cause this much damage. The Tri-State Tornado is still the deadliest tornado on record. There wasn't much warning, so most people were caught by surprise.

Today, we have better ways to warn people about tornadoes. Using computers and radar, scientists can predict tornadoes 12 to 48 hours in advance. The U.S. Weather Service issues a tornado watch. The watch is upgraded to a warning when a funnel cloud is reported, or if other conditions occur. Even so, tornadoes are one of the most violent kinds of storms in the world.

Photo courtesy of the National Oceanic and Atmospheric Administration/Department of Commerce

Find It!

Read the spelling words.
Check off the words you can find in the story.

- [x] believe
- [x] people
- [ ] lightning
- [x] explode
- [ ] freight
- [ ] piece
- [ ] weigh
- [x] which
- [ ] fact
- [x] damage
- [x] violent
- [x] tornado

How many spelling words did you find? _____

Skills:

ie and **ei**
Spelling
Patterns

Silent **gh**

Visual Memory

Spelling
Theme
Vocabulary

Spelling Practice

Read and Spell	Copy and Spell	Spell It Again!
1. believe	believe	believe
2. people	people	people
3. lightning	lightning	lightning
4. explode	explode	explode
5. freight	freight	freight
6. piece	piece	piece
7. weigh	weigh	weigh
8. damage	damage	damage
9. which	which	which
10. violent	violent	violent
11. tornado	tornado	torndo
12. fact	fact	fact

Write It Right

Skills:

Editing for Spelling

Visual Memory

Writing Spelling Words

ie and **ei** Spelling Patterns

Silent **gh**

Circle the misspelled spelling words in the sentences. Write the words correctly on the lines.

1. Some ~~peeple~~ are afraid of thunder and lightning storms.

   _____ People _____

2. Tanya could not choose ~~whitch~~ sport to play.

   _____ which _____

3. The tornado caused a lot of ~~damige~~ to the town.

   _____ damage _____

4. Caitlin watched the fireworks ~~exploid~~ in the night sky.

   _____ explode _____

5. Tham researched each ~~fac~~ before writing her report.

   _____ fact _____

6. The workers had to weigh the ~~freigt~~ before loading it.

   _____ freight _____

7. Jerome could not ~~beleiv~~ he had really won the race.

   _____ believe _____

8. Hurricanes are ~~violint~~ storms that form over the ocean.

   _____

9. Please save me a ~~piese~~ of that chocolate cake.

   _____ piece _____

Match the Meanings

Write the spelling word for each definition.

believe	people	lightning	explode
freight	piece	weigh	which
fact	damage	violent	tornado

1. a part of a whole _____

2. human beings _____

3. showing great force; furious _____

4. to burst noisily or violently _____

5. the harm something does _____

6. a piece of true information _____

7. a flash of light from a discharge of electricity _____

8. to accept as true or real _____

9. the one or ones mentioned _____

10. to figure out the heaviness of an object _____

11. goods to be shipped _____

12. a violent funnel-shaped windstorm _____

Search for Sentences

▶ **There are four types of sentences:**

- declarative — makes a statement—ends with a period (.)
- interrogative — asks a question—ends with a question mark (?)
- imperative — makes a command—ends with a period (.)
- exclamatory — shows strong feeling—ends with an exclamation point (!)

Fill in the circle the correct name for each sentence.

1. We watched the tree explode as lightning struck

○ declarative
○ interrogative
○ imperative
○ exclamatory

2. Wow, look at all that damage

○ declarative
○ interrogative
○ imperative
○ exclamatory

3. The storm sounded like a freight train rushing by

○ declarative
○ interrogative
○ imperative
○ exclamatory

4. Which kind of storm is the most violent

○ declarative
○ interrogative
○ imperative
○ exclamatory

5. Clean up the debris in the yard right now

○ declarative
○ interrogative
○ imperative
○ exclamatory

6. Are hurricanes as violent as tornadoes

○ declarative
○ interrogative
○ imperative
○ exclamatory

Finish the Story

believe	people	lightning	explode
freight	piece	weigh	which
fact	damage	violent	tornado

Complete the story using words from the spelling list. One word will not be used.

One warm, stormy day in April, flashes of _____ lit the sky. I went out onto the porch. The air was still and seemed to _____ heavily on me. It was waiting for something to happen.

When I turned on the radio, I couldn't _____ what I heard. _____ had spotted a large funnel cloud, a _____. I knew exactly what to do. I kept the radio on to hear news as it came in. I wondered how _____ this tornado might be, and how much _____ might result.

First, I had to stay away from windows that might _____ during the storm. I also knew _____ places were safest to hide. I could go into the basement or a downstairs bathroom or closet. I would know when the tornado was coming. It would sound as loud as a _____ train.

I waited for a long time. Finally, the _____ of information I was waiting for came over the radio. The tornado warning had been reduced to a watch. The funnel cloud had disappeared!

Spellamadoodle

Write each spelling word on the outline of the drawing. You may use the words more than once. For fun, decorate the picture.

believe	people	lightning	explode
freight	piece	weigh	which
fact	damage	violent	tornado

Poetry Time

Create an acrostic poem. Write a word or phrase that starts with each letter in the topic word. Use words in the story to help you.

T _____

O _____

R _____

N _____

A _____

D _____

O _____

Read All About It!

Write a lead paragraph for a newspaper article about a tornado that ripped through your town. Describe all the things you heard, saw, and felt. Be sure to add a headline that will grab your readers' attention. Use at least four spelling words in your article.

believe	people	lightning	explode
freight	piece	weigh	which
fact	damage	violent	tornado

OUR TOP STORY

_____

_____

_____   _____

_____   _____

_____   _____

_____   _____

_____   _____

_____   _____

_____   _____

The Daily News

✔ Edit Your Work

○ I used complete sentences.

○ I used correct spelling.

○ I used correct capitalization and punctuation.

Wild Winds

Spelling Test

Find the correct answer. Fill in the circle.

1. Which kind of sentence is this?

   Watch out for that window

   ○ interrogative
   ○ declarative
   ○ exclamatory

2. Which punctuation mark should go at the end of this sentence?

   Did they issue a tornado warning

   ○ exclamation point (!)
   ○ question mark (?)
   ○ period (.)

3. Which word is spelled correctly?

   ○ peopul
   ○ people
   ○ poeple

4. Which word means "to figure out the heaviness of an object"?

   ○ fact
   ○ piece
   ○ weigh

Ask someone to test you on the spelling words.

1. _____

2. _____

3. _____

4. _____

5. _____

6. _____

7. _____

8. _____

9. _____

10. _____

11. _____

12. _____

5. Write the sentence correctly.

   i beleive this tornadoe is the most violint I've ever seen

   _____

   _____

Comets

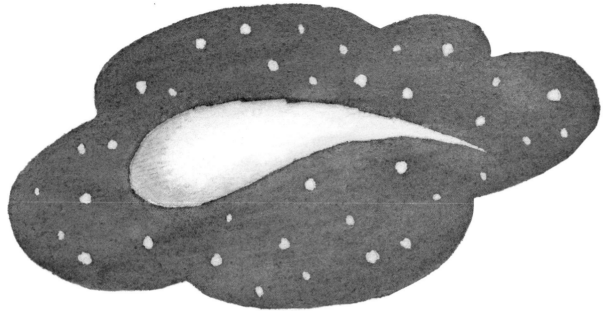

Have you ever seen a comet streak across the night sky? Many people used to think that comets were on fire. Now we know that comets are frozen lumps of ice and dust. They enter our solar system from far away. When a comet gets close to the sun, the sun's heat vaporizes some of the comet. Gas and dust are released and form long sunlit tails that follow the comet. We can see these beautiful tails, which can be millions of miles long, from Earth.

Comet comes from a Greek word meaning "long-haired star." This is because the tail of the comet looks like flowing hair.

The most famous comet is Halley's comet. Reports of this comet date back more than 2,200 years! Halley's comet makes its usual visit every 76 years. If you want to see Halley's comet, you'll have to wait a long time. It won't visit Earth again until 2061, many years in the future.

Find It!

Read the spelling words.
Check off the words you can find in the story.

☐ collide	☑ million	☐ matter	☑ across
☐ follow	☐ litter	☑ future	☑ usual
☑ used	☑ beautiful	☑ year	☐ cause

How many spelling words did you find? _____

Skills:

Double
Consonants

Long **u**

Visual Memory

Spelling
Theme
Vocabulary

Spelling Practice

Read and Spell	Copy and Spell	Spell It Again!
1. collide	collide	collide
2. million	million	million
3. matter	matter	matter
4. across	across	across
5. follow	follow	follow
6. litter	litter	liter
7. future	future	future
8. usual	usual	usual
9. used	used	used
10. beautiful	beautiful	beaatifal
11. year	year	year
12. cause	cause	cause

Crossword Challenge

Complete the crossword puzzle using the spelling words.

collide	million	matter	across
follow	litter	future	usual
used	beautiful	year	cause

Across

2. to go behind
4. clutter; objects that are strewn about
6. all things that contain atoms and take up space
9. common; expected
10. to make something happen

Down

1. to crash together with great force
3. very pretty
5. from one side to the other
6. a large number
7. time not yet here
8. a unit of time equal to about 365 days
9. to put into action

Search and Spell

Circle the word in each row that is spelled correctly.

1. (beatiful)   beautiful   beutiful

2. folow   folloe   (follow)

3. milion   (million)   milleon

4. (across)   acros   accross

5. yeer   yeare   (year)

6. ussual   (usual)   usuall

7. cawse   causse   (cause)

8. (matter)   mater   mattar

Use the spelling word *collide* in a sentence.

_____

_____

Use the spelling word *future* in a sentence.

__I wate to be a vet__

__in The future__

Simple and Compound Sentences

▶ A simple sentence expresses one complete thought. It has a subject and a verb.

Our solar system | has nine planets.
   (subject)   (verb)

A compound sentence is two or more simple sentences put together.

- The parts are usually joined by a conjunction such as *and*, *or*, or *but*.
- A comma is placed before the conjunction.

> Manned spacecraft have landed on the moon, but none have landed on Mars.

Write *S* for simple or *C* for compound. Circle the conjunctions.

1. An asteroid is made of rock, and a comet is made of ice and dust. _____

2. I saw the shooting star, but no one else saw it. _____

3. There are millions of stars in the sky. _____

4. An asteroid may have killed the dinosaurs, but no one is sure. _____

5. Meteoroids can come from asteroids, or they can come from comets. _____

Write a simple sentence and a compound sentence about space rocks.

1. _____

_____

2. _____

_____

Word Search

Find and circle the spelling words. Words can go across, down, or diagonally.

used	beautiful	usual	year
matter	follow	million	cause
future	across	collide	litter

```
L U L I L I E B E U C M I U U
A I E U I S I O T U L O O T T
L S I I U B E A U T I F U L T
A C F A T T R C M U F E D E B
F T C L D I S R R C O Y L R O
L U F M R I U U E M T S E F R
M O T M A T T E R I M L O A E
L U F U N E A L L L E A U C R
E T T S R R T L A L Y S I T E
R A E F F E E E U I T D R L D
F O L L O W R S S O U I E L L
A F T E E D F F U N S O T S I
F L A C R O S S F U R O T L U
R I A E W O O U S R I E I L R
A F C O L L I D E D R B L E L
I L E L U U C L U S A Y L F L
```

Spellamadoodle

Write each spelling word on the outline of the drawing. You may use the words more than once. For fun, decorate the picture.

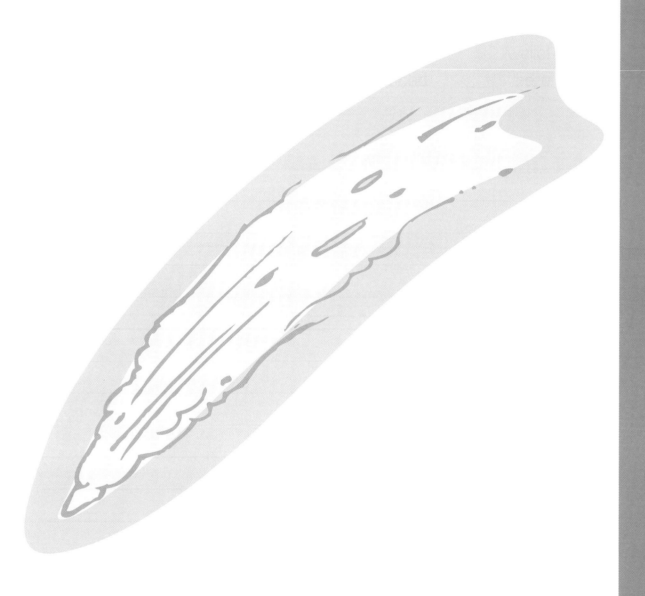

collide	million	matter	across
follow	litter	future	usual
used	beautiful	year	cause

Skills:

Using Spelling
Words in
an Original
Composition

Writing
Sentences

Writing
Spelling Words

A Day of Discovery

Write a short story about discovering a comet. Use specific, interesting adjectives to describe what the comet looks like. What will you name it? Use at least six spelling words in your writing.

collide	million	matter	across
follow	litter	future	usual
used	beautiful	year	cause

_____

_____

_____

_____

_____

_____

_____

_____

_____

_____

_____

✓ **Edit Your Work**

○ I used complete sentences.

○ I used correct spelling.

○ I used correct capitalization and punctuation.

Cinquains in Space

Skills:

Using Spelling
Words in
Poetry

Writing
Spelling Words

A **cinquain** is a five-line poem with a specific number of words.

Line 1: Write a one-word subject.
Line 2: Write two words describing the subject.
Line 3: Write three action words about the subject.
Line 4: Write a four-word statement about the subject.
Line 5: Write one word that refers back to the subject.

Example: Meteor
           Bright, fast
           Streaking, shooting, blazing
           Through the night sky
           Rock

Write a cinquain about a comet, asteroid, star, or planet in the frame below. Use at least two spelling words in your cinquain. Look back at the story to help you.

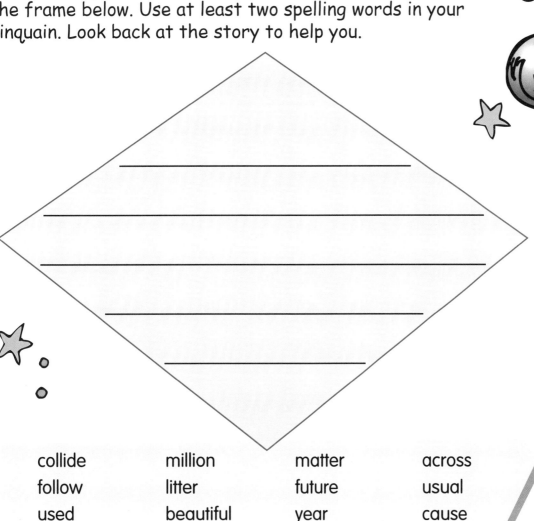

collide	million	matter	across
follow	litter	future	usual
used	beautiful	year	cause

TEST YOUR SKILLS — Comets

Spelling Test

Find the correct answer. Fill in the circle.

1. Which of the following is a simple sentence?
   - ○ I like watching stars, so I bought a telescope.
   - ○ I saw a shooting star from my window last night.
   - ○ The comet had long tail, and it shone beautifully last night.

2. Which of the following is a compound sentence?
   - ○ Our universe is littered with space rocks.
   - ○ Comets are made of ice and dust, and when they near the sun, glowing tails form.
   - ○ An asteroid may have hit Earth 65 million years ago.

3. Which word is spelled correctly?
   - ○ fuchure
   - ○ future
   - ○ fuchur

4. Which word means "common" or "expected"?
   - ○ usual
   - ○ across
   - ○ cause

Ask someone to test you on the spelling words.

1. _____
2. _____
3. _____
4. _____
5. _____
6. _____
7. _____
8. _____
9. _____
10. _____
11. _____
12. _____

5. Write the sentence correctly.

   milions of asteroids colide each year and this causes more mattur to liter space

   _____

   _____

The Greeks Were First

The Olympic Games have been around a long time! The ancient games began in Greece in 776 B.C. At first, the games were a holiday in honor of Zeus. He was the father of all the Greek gods. The games were held at Mt. Olympus, the highest mountain in Greece. They took place every fourth summer in July or August.

Athletes did not compete on teams, but as individuals. Only men and boys could compete. They trained for ten long months. Before the games began, they swore an oath of honesty. Their fathers and brothers had to swear the same oath.

Some events were similar to today's events. There were foot races, wrestling, boxing, jumping, and javelin throwing. There were also different events, such as chariot races. The biggest difference was the dress. Athletes competed without clothes!

Winners did not get medals. Instead, they were given wreaths of olive leaves. Winning athletes were hailed as great heroes. They became rich and famous. Poems and sculptures were created in their honor.

Where were the women and girls? Women were not allowed to compete. They weren't even allowed to watch! There was another festival to honor Hera, the wife of Zeus. That event had foot races for unmarried girls.

Find It! Read the spelling words.
Check off the words you can find in the story.

☐ ancient	☐ oath	☐ heroes	☐ swore
☐ brother	☐ holiday	☐ athlete	☐ mountain
☐ month	☐ July	☐ August	☐ summer

How many spelling words did you find? _____

Spelling Practice

Read and Spell	Copy and Spell	Spell It Again!

1. ancient   _____   _____

2. oath   _____   _____

3. heroes   _____   _____

4. swore   _____   _____

5. brother   _____   _____

6. holiday   _____   _____

7. athlete   _____   _____

8. mountain   _____   _____

9. month   _____   _____

10. July   _____   _____

11. August   _____   _____

12. summer   _____   _____

On Target

Skills:

Editing for Spelling

Visual Discrimination

Writing Spelling Words

Spelling Words with the Vowel **o**

Spelling Names of Months

Circle the word in each row that is spelled correctly.

1. oathe   oeth   oath

2. mountin   montain   mountain

3. swore   swoar   swor

4. heroes   heros   herros

5. brothur   bruther   brother

6. ancient   anchent   aincent

7. summur   sumer   summer

8. athleet   athlete   athlet

Circle the misspelled words in the sentences. Write them correctly on the lines.

1. My favorite holliday is the Fourth of Juli.

_____

_____

2. Agust is the munth in which I was born.

_____

_____

Word Search

Find and circle the spelling words. Words can go across, down, or diagonally.

ancient	oath	heroes	swore
brother	holiday	athlete	mountain
month	July	August	summer

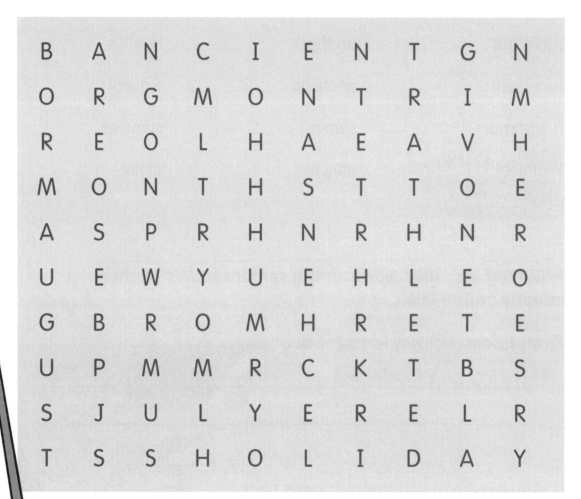

```
B  A  N  C  I  E  N  T  G  N
O  R  G  M  O  N  T  R  I  M
R  E  O  L  H  A  E  A  V  H
M  O  N  T  H  S  T  T  O  E
A  S  P  R  H  N  R  H  N  R
U  E  W  Y  U  E  H  L  E  O
G  B  R  O  M  H  R  E  T  E
U  P  M  M  R  C  K  T  B  S
S  J  U  L  Y  E  R  E  L  R
T  S  S  H  O  L  I  D  A  Y
```

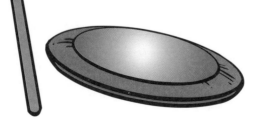

Pronoun Puzzler

A pronoun is used in place of a noun.

I   you   he   she   they   it   me   him   her   us   them

| Tia loves pizza. | Nathan and Manuel are best friends. |
| She loves pizza. | They are best friends. |

Replace the underlined words with a pronoun. Rewrite the sentence. The first one has been done for you.

1. Milo of Kroton loved to show off for people.

   <u>He loved to show off for them.</u>

2. A man would use horses for chariot races.

   _____

3. Greek legend says that Hera and Zeus lived on Mt. Olympus.

   _____

4. Mt. Olympus was where the Olympics took place.

   _____

5. A woman was not allowed to compete in the games.

   _____

6. A man could compete in any of the events.

   _____

7. The athletes had to swear an oath before playing.

   _____

8. The Greeks were the first to celebrate the Olympic Games.

   _____

Poetry Time

Create an acrostic poem. Write a word or phrase that starts with each letter in the topic word. Use words in the story to help you.

O _____

L _____

Y _____

M _____

P _____

I _____

C _____

S _____

Spell & Write • EMC 4540 • © Evan-Moor Corporation

Spellamadoodle

Write each spelling word on the outline of the drawing. You may use the words more than once. For fun, decorate the drawing.

ancient	oath	heroes	sworn
brother	holiday	athlete	mountain
month	July	August	summer

Diagoras the Noble

Complete the story using words from the spelling list.

ancient	oath	heroes	swore
brother	holiday	athlete	mountain
month	July	August	summer

There were many _____ of the _____ Olympic games. One hero was a boxer named Diagoras of Rhodes. He was known as a noble _____. Some even _____ he was the son of the god Hermes.

The famous poet Pindar wrote of Diagoras' great skills. He praised Diagoras as huge, strong, and fair. During the hot _____ of the 79th Olympics, Diagoras won many victories. He became a legend in his own time.

Winning was all in the family for Diagoras. He even lived to see his sons win Olympic victories. In 448 B.C., one of his sons won the pancratium. This event was a mix of boxing and wrestling. His _____ won in boxing. The excited crowd celebrated this special _____ by showering the men with flowers.

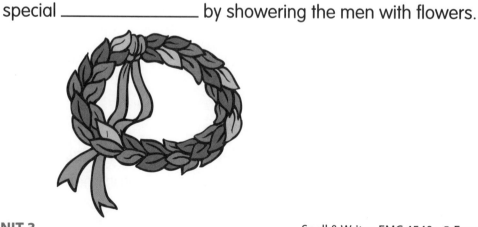

Ode to a Hero

A statue has been built for a famous Olympic athlete. You are an ancient Greek writer. You have been hired to write words for a special plaque. Describe this athlete's great skill and strength. Use some of the spelling words in your writing.

ancient	oath	heroes	swore
brother	holiday	athlete	mountain
month	July	August	summer

Edit Your Work

○ I used complete sentences.

○ I used correct spelling.

○ I used correct capitalization and punctuation.

Find the correct answer. Fill in the circle.

1. Which set of pronouns should replace the underlined words in this sentence?

   <u>A girl</u> could run in a foot race in honor of <u>Hera</u>, queen of the gods.

   ○ She, her

   ○ Her, him

   ○ He, they

2. Which set of pronouns should replace the underlined words in this sentence?

   <u>Diagoras' sons</u> won <u>Olympic victories</u>.

   ○ She, them

   ○ He, it

   ○ They, them

3. Which word is spelled correctly?

   ○ montain

   ○ mountain

   ○ mountaine

4. Which word is spelled correctly?

   ○ athlete

   ○ athelete

   ○ athleet

Ask someone to test you on the spelling words.

1. _____

2. _____

3. _____

4. _____

5. _____

6. _____

7. _____

8. _____

9. _____

10. _____

11. _____

12. _____

5. Write the sentence correctly.

   the sommer munths of Juli and Agust were the times of ancient Olympic games

   _____

   _____

Word Search

Find and circle the spelling words. Words can go across, down, or diagonally.

they're	don't	couldn't	aren't
who's	everything	everyone	anyone
anything	temperature	through	curious

```
T E H U N A N Y O N E M Y A G
N R D C O U L D N T T Y T T N
E V E R Y O N E E H N E T E N
R G T C M H U I R T W T Y T R
U T R U N S O O O H U O I N R
T T R H O H U S Y T E O É O R
A C I I L G O N U Y E S R D U
R U R T H H A R S E H P D R P
E R E I W G E Y E R S A A Y T
P I O A E V E R Y T H I N G D
M O N N R G E R Y T H H E Y E
E U A E H E N W H E V T T R E
T S E E N T N R U E H N A Y T
P T H O N Y A T H I Y T C H V
I N A N Y T H I N G E E E V O
```

An Interview

Interview someone you know who has an unusual pet, such as a snake or chinchilla. If you don't know anyone, interview someone who would like to have an unusual pet.

1. What is the name of your unusual pet?

_____

2. Where does the animal come from?

_____

_____

3. What food does the animal eat?

_____

_____

4. What special care does the animal need?

_____

_____

_____

5. Name three things that make this pet unusual.

_____

_____

_____

The Perfect Pet

What kind of unusual pet would you like to own? Would you own some kind of wild animal or reptile? Describe your perfect, unusual pet. Describe how you would care for it. Give it a name. Use as many spelling words as you can.

they're	don't	couldn't	aren't
who's	everything	everyone	anyone
anything	through	curious	temperature

_____

_____

_____

_____

_____

_____

_____

_____

_____

_____

Draw a picture of your unusual pet.

✓ Edit Your Work

○ I used complete sentences.

○ I used correct spelling.

○ I used correct capitalization and punctuation.

Unusual Pets

Find the correct answer. Fill in the circle.

1. Which word shows possession correctly?
    - ○ Jamies' baseball
    - ○ Mia's' tarantula
    - ○ the woman's coat

2. Which word shows possession correctly?
    - ○ our family's pets
    - ○ the pigs ears
    - ○ the skun'ks tail

3. Which word is spelled correctly?
    - ○ tempature
    - ○ temperature
    - ○ temperture

4. Which word means "eager to find out"?
    - ○ cannibal
    - ○ couldn't
    - ○ curious

Spelling Test

Ask someone to test you on the spelling words.

1. _____

2. _____

3. _____

4. _____

5. _____

6. _____

7. _____

8. _____

9. _____

10. _____

11. _____

12. _____

5. Write the sentence correctly.

    they'er curios about snakes, but they dont know anething about feeding them

    _____

    _____

They Changed the World

Thomas Edison

Have you ever tried reading by the light of a candle? It's not easy! We don't even think about it when we switch on a light. But before electric light, people used only candles. Thomas Edison worked on the electric light bulb for two years. He tried to make it work more than 1,000 times. In 1879, he found success! This invention made Edison famous around the world. He also worked on other things such as the telephone and typewriter. He held over 1,000 patents for his inventions!

The Wright Brothers

People have always wanted to fly. The Wright brothers were the first to make it happen. The date was December 17, 1903. The place was Kitty Hawk, North Carolina. In a plane made of wood, cotton, and cloth, the Wright brothers made the very first flights. Their famous plane, *Flyer*, started a new era. Since then, flight has become one of the quickest and most common ways of traveling. For decades, thousands of people have traveled on jets around the world. Every year, flights become quicker.

Find It!

Read the spelling words.
Check off the words you can find in the story.

lived	living	traveled	traveling
changed	changing	earlier	earliest
quicker	quickest	telephone	light

How many spelling words did you find? _____

Spelling Practice

Read and Spell	Copy and Spell	Spell It Again!

1. lived

2. living

3. traveled

4. traveling

5. changed

6. changing

7. earlier

8. earliest

9. quicker

10. quickest

11. telephone

12. light

Spelling in Sentences

Choose the correct spelling. Write the word on the line.

1. People who **livd/lived** long ago used candles for light.

   _____

2. Flying is one of the **quikist/quickest** ways to travel.

   _____

3. New inventions keep things **changing/changeing**.

   _____

4. Have you ever **traveled/travled** on a jet?

   _____

5. Bell invented what we know as the **telephone/telafone**.

   _____

6. The **earlyist/earliest** flight took place in Kitty Hawk.

   _____

7. Electric **light/ligte** was invented by Edison.

   _____

8. My parents are **travling/traveling** to Europe by jet.

   _____

9. Cars have **chanjed/changed** a lot since 1910.

   _____

10. The car was invented **erlier/earlier** than the plane.

    _____

Finish It

Fix these sentences. Use spelling words to replace the underlined words.

lived	living	traveled	traveling
changed	changing	earlier	earliest
quicker	quickest	telephone	light

1. We are <u>change</u> flights in New York.

_____

2. A car is the <u>quick</u> way to get around the city.

_____

3. The telephone was invented <u>early</u> than I thought.

_____

4. The Wright brothers' longest flight <u>travel</u> 852 feet.

_____

5. A plane is <u>quick</u> than a train.

_____

6. Some people think <u>live</u> in the past would be fun.

_____

7. The Wright brothers flew one of the <u>early</u> planes.

_____

8. My family loves <u>travel</u> to new places.

_____

Action or Linking?

Action verbs **tell what the subject is doing.**

Maya kicked the soccer ball.

Linking verbs **link a subject to a noun or an adjective that names or describes the subject.**

His (shirt) is blue with white stripes.

The (lion) looks sleepy lying under the tree.

Circle the verb in each sentence.
Write A for action or L for linking on the line.

1. Sara's book is about great inventions. _____

2. The book looks thicker than an encyclopedia. _____

3. I heard the telephone this morning. _____

4. Next time, call earlier than 10:00 a.m. _____

5. This route is the quickest. _____

6. Jason traveled across the country by train. _____

7. Miranda lives near the train tracks. _____

8. The Wright brothers were ahead of their time. _____

9. Edison's electric light changed the world. _____

10. Many great inventions came even earlier. _____

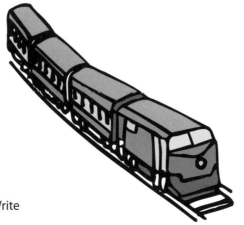

Skills:

Writing
Spelling Words

Using Spelling
Words in
Poetry

Cinquain of Change

A **cinquain** is a five-line poem with a specific number of words.

Line 1: Write a one-word subject.
Line 2: Write two words describing the subject.
Line 3: Write three action words about the subject.
Line 4: Write a four-word statement about the subject.
Line 5: Write one word that refers back to the subject.

Write a cinquain about your favorite invention.

Spellamadoodle

Write each spelling word on the outline of the drawing. You may use the words more than once. For fun, decorate the drawing.

lived	living	traveled	traveling
changed	changing	earlier	earliest
quicker	quickest	telephone	light

Skills:

Writing a
Description

Using Spelling
Words in a
Composition

Great Inventions

Imagine you are a famous inventor like the Wright brothers or Thomas Edison. You have invented something that will change the world. What is your invention? What is it called? What does it do? Describe your invention below. Use as many spelling words as you can.

lived	living	traveled	traveling
changed	changing	earlier	earliest
quicker	quickest	telephone	light

_____

_____

_____

_____

Draw a picture of your invention.

_____

_____

_____

_____

_____

_____

_____

_____

_____

✓ **Edit Your Work**

◯ I used complete sentences.

◯ I used correct spelling.

◯ I used correct capitalization and punctuation.

The Good Old Days

Talk with an older person about what life was like when he or she was young. Ask the questions below. Then answer the second set of questions yourself. Compare your answers.

Then	Now
1. When were you born? _____ _____	I was born _____ _____
2. What was your favorite toy or game? _____ _____	My favorite toy or game is _____ _____
3. What music did you like? _____ _____	The music I like is _____ _____
4. What kinds of clothes did you wear? _____ _____	I like to wear _____ _____
5. What has changed the most since you were young? _____ _____	Since I was a baby, what has changed the most is _____ _____

Find the correct answer. Fill in the circle.

1. Which word in this sentence is the action verb?

   Hector laughed at the dolphin's funny tricks.

   ○ tricks
   ○ funny
   ○ laughed

2. Which word in this sentence is the linking verb?

   These cookies are better than the cake.

   ○ are
   ○ better
   ○ cake

3. Which word is spelled correctly?

   ○ telefone
   ○ teluphone
   ○ telephone

4. Which word means "alive now"?

   ○ living
   ○ lived
   ○ liver

Ask someone to test you on the spelling words.

1. _____

2. _____

3. _____

4. _____

5. _____

6. _____

7. _____

8. _____

9. _____

10. _____

11. _____

12. _____

5. Write the sentence correctly.

   the telaphon was the erliest and quikest change in the way people talked to each other

   _____

   _____

The Buried City: Pompeii

In 91 B.C., Pompeii was a great port city in southern Italy. Pompeii was built on the slopes of Mt. Vesuvius. It had a view of the sea. It was also a resort town, rich with fine goods. The people of Pompeii did not know that they sat at the feet of a sleeping giant.

In 800 B.C., Mt. Vesuvius was an active volcano. It erupted many times. But by 91 B.C., Mt. Vesuvius had been sleeping for almost 800 years. The people of Pompeii had no idea that one of the worst disasters in history was about to occur.

In A.D. 79, the awesome mountain began to rumble. The earth shook. People looked up in wonder. Showers of hot ash and awful poison gas filled the air. Mud and lava raced toward the city. The people of Pompeii were trapped. In a matter of hours, the city was buried. Most people escaped. But more than 2,000 were left behind.

It wasn't until the 1700s that people began to dig up the buried city. Under nine feet of packed ash, they found "shells" (or molds) of people and animals who had been buried. Today, you can visit Pompeii and see these molds. You can also see artwork and buildings thousands of years old.

Find It!

Read the spelling words.
Check off the words you can find in the story.

☐ also	☐ almost	☐ awful	☐ awesome
☐ early	☐ earth	☐ wonder	☐ shower
☐ world	☐ worst	☐ volcano	☐ erupt

How many spelling words did you find? _____

Skills:

Spelling
Words with
R-Controlled
Vowels (**er, or, ear**)

Spelling Words
with **ô**

Spelling
Theme
Vocabulary

Visual Memory

Spelling Practice

Read and Spell	Copy and Spell	Spell It Again!
1. also	_____	_____
2. almost	_____	_____
3. awful	_____	_____
4. awesome	_____	_____
5. early	_____	_____
6. earth	_____	_____
7. wonder	_____	_____
8. shower	_____	_____
9. world	_____	_____
10. worst	_____	_____
11. volcano	_____	_____
12. erupt	_____	_____

Crossword Challenge

Skills:

Matching
Words
with Their
Meanings

Writing
Spelling Words

Visual Memory

Complete the crossword puzzle using the spelling words.

Across

2. terrible; very bad
4. the ground
6. very nearly
9. mountain that erupts with ash and lava
10. amazing; creates awe
12. to explode with great force

Down

1. most harmful or unpleasant
3. the Earth, or another name for it
5. as well
7. to fall in large numbers
8. at or near the beginning
11. surprise; amazement

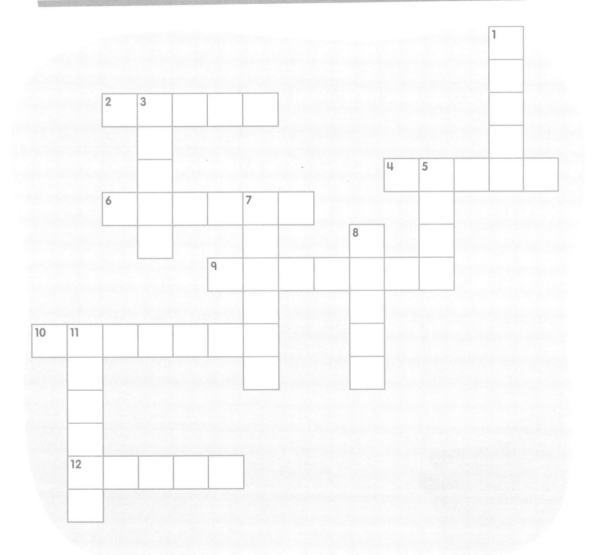

Word Search

Find and circle the spelling words. Words can go across, down, or diagonally.

also	almost	awful	awesome
early	earth	wonder	shower
world	worst	volcano	erupt

```
P  E  T  U  P  A  W  F  U  L  O  C
B  R  A  A  N  V  E  T  K  R  U  R
S  Y  O  R  B  W  S  I  X  O  T  H
V  O  T  S  H  O  W  E  R  O  S  W
C  O  A  P  M  N  R  O  I  W  E  O
E  G  L  L  Y  D  O  A  R  I  S  R
A  W  A  C  C  E  W  V  A  L  M  S
R  E  T  E  A  R  T  H  A  I  D  T
L  E  A  R  O  N  K  A  L  G  O  N
Y  W  R  U  T  C  O  T  U  U  L  M
W  E  A  P  R  O  S  S  D  A  E  E
I  T  S  T  A  W  E  S  O  M  E  S
```

Spell & Write • EMC 4540 • © Evan-Moor Corporation

Present, Past, or Future?

The tense of a verb tells when an action occurs. Endings or helping verbs are added to change the tense.

- present—The action is happening now.

    Mina talks to her best friend.
- past—The action already happened.

    Mina talked to her best friend.
- future—The action is going to happen.

    Mina will talk to her best friend.

Circle the correct form of the verb.

1. The volcano **erupted/will erupt** in five days.

2. Even now, Jamie **climbs/climbed** volcanoes every summer.

3. Brad **enjoys/will enjoy** reading this volcano book tomorrow.

4. I **watched/watch** the eruption yesterday.

5. Tham constantly **researches/will research** Pompeii.

6. Ash and gas **shower/showered** into the air in 91 B.C.

Spellamadoodle

Write each spelling word on the outline of the drawing. You may use the words more than once. For fun, decorate the drawing.

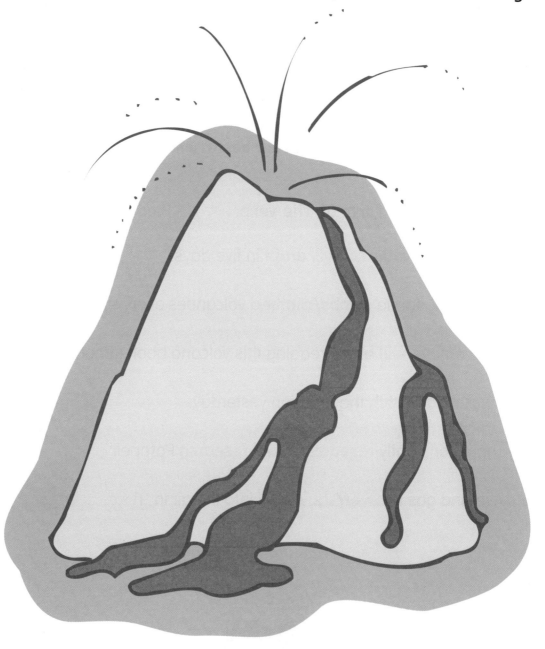

also	almost	awful	awesome
early	earth	wonder	shower
world	worst	volcano	erupt

Poetry Time

Create an acrostic poem. Write a word or phrase that starts with
each letter in the topic word. Use the words in the story
to help you.

V _____

O _____

L _____

C _____

A _____

N _____

O _____

Skills:

Using Context
Clues to
Identify
Missing
Spelling Words

Writing
Spelling Words

Mount St. Helens

Complete the story using words from the spelling list. One word will not be used.

also	almost	awful	awesome
early	earth	wonder	shower
world	worst	volcano	erupt

It was May 18, 1980, in Washington State. Something

_____ was about to happen! _____ on

this Sunday morning, Mount St. Helens sprang into action. No one

thought this sleeping _____ could _____.

First, the _____ shook with a large earthquake. Then, this

_____ volcano began spewing a _____ of

ash and lava into the air. _____ the entire north face of

the mountain collapsed. This was the _____ eruption that

had happened in years. Nearly 150 square miles of land was destroyed.

The volcano continues to erupt off and on. Now, this beautiful

place is _____ a national monument. You can visit the park.

It's a _____ to see!

>>>>>>>>>>>>>>>>>>>>>>>>>>>>>>>>>>>>>

This Is How It Happened

You are a TV reporter sent to report on the eruption of a volcano. This newly discovered volcano has been exploding for several hours. Describe what you see, hear, and smell. Use as many spelling words as you can. Then read your report aloud, as if you are on TV!

also	almost	awful	awesome
early	earth	wonder	shower
world	worst	volcano	erupt

✓ Edit Your Work

○ I used complete sentences.

○ I used correct spelling.

○ I used correct capitalization and punctuation.

Find the correct answer. Fill in the circle.

1. Is the verb in this sentence present, past, or future tense?

   Tia travels the world to visit volcanoes.

   ○ present
   ○ past
   ○ future

2. Is the verb in this sentence present, past, or future tense?

   Mai Le will write about the volcano's next eruption.

   ○ present
   ○ past
   ○ future

3. Which word is spelled correctly?

   ○ wurst
   ○ whorst
   ○ worst

4. Which word means "surprise" or "amazement"?

   ○ wonder
   ○ shower
   ○ world

Spelling Test

Ask someone to test you on the spelling words.

1. _____

2. _____

3. _____

4. _____

5. _____

6. _____

7. _____

8. _____

9. _____

10. _____

11. _____

12. _____

5. Write the sentence correctly.

   jake will tell us that the world's most awsome vollcano will eropt soon

   _____

   _____

Rainforest Frogs

Poison dart frogs are easy to recognize by their bright colors. They can be yellow, blue, red, green, or orange. These colors are a clue to other animals that the frog is poisonous. Dart frogs are beautiful, but dangerous. They have poison glands all over their bodies. When frightened, the frog oozes deadly poison from its skin. Because of this, dart frogs have few enemies. Their poison is known as one of the most toxic in the world. Some native tribes choose this poison for dart tips when hunting. One frog can make enough poison for 50 darts!

The red-eyed tree frog is gentler than its larger cousin. This tiny frog is smaller than your finger, only one to two inches long. With suction cups on its toes, the red-eyed tree frog can attach itself to leaves and trees.

This helps it hunt for its favorite treats—flies, moths, and grasshoppers. One way this frog protects itself is by using its strange red eyes. If an enemy is near, the frog closes and then quickly opens them. Its giant red eyes scare the other animal so much that it runs away!

Find It! Read the spelling words.
Check off the words you can find in the story.

☐ few	☐ blue	☐ clue	☐ choose
☐ ooze	☐ dangerous	☐ gentle	☐ strange
☐ giant	☐ poison	☐ cousin	☐ toxic

How many spelling words did you find? _____

Spelling Practice

Read and Spell	Copy and Spell	Spell It Again!
1. few	_____	_____
2. blue	_____	_____
3. clue	_____	_____
4. choose	_____	_____
5. ooze	_____	_____
6. dangerous	_____	_____
7. gentle	_____	_____
8. strange	_____	_____
9. giant	_____	_____
10. poison	_____	_____
11. cousin	_____	_____
12. toxic	_____	_____

Sound and Meaning

Which spelling word means the same as ... ?

few	blue	clue	choose
ooze	dangerous	gentle	strange
giant	poison	cousin	toxic

1. to select _____

2. kind, sensitive _____

3. likely to harm _____

4. odd _____

5. huge _____

6. to flow out slowly _____

7. not many _____

8. harmful substance _____

9. color of the sky _____

10. child of your aunt or uncle _____

11. hint _____

12. poisonous _____

Skills:

Editing for Spelling

Spelling Words with **oo**

Spelling Words with **g** and **j**

Spelling Theme Vocabulary

Visual Memory

Circle the misspelled word in each sentence. Write the word correctly on the line.

1. Some frogs are small, and some are jiant. _____

2. Some animals use danjerious poison to defend themselves. _____

3. The blue dart frog is a coussin to the red-eyed tree frog. _____

4. A frog's poison will oose out of its skin. _____

5. Many animals choose to stay away from these toxick frogs. _____

6. The tree frog scares enemies away with its stranje red eyes. _____

7. Fue people can count all the animals in the rainforest. _____

8. Bright colors are a clew that animals might be poisonous. _____

9. The red-eyed tree frog is more gentil than the dart frog. _____

10. Dart frogs can be blu, yellow, red, green, or orange. _____

Word Search

Find and circle the spelling words. Words can go across, down,
or diagonally.

```
P  O  I  S  O  N  H  I  S  T
D  A  C  W  V  W  G  J  R  C
H  A  K  I  V  Y  E  Z  O  O
I  G  N  X  X  Z  F  F  Q  U
J  F  L  G  T  O  E  K  P  S
E  E  M  I  E  A  T  L  O  I
L  D  N  A  S  R  D  C  N  N
T  C  O  N  R  B  O  L  M  U
N  B  P  T  Q  C  E  U  L  B
E  G  N  A  R  T  S  E  S  V
G  A  R  D  E  S  O  O  H  C
```

few	blue	clue	choose
ooze	dangerous	gentle	strange
giant	poison	cousin	toxic

Describing Words

A **noun** names a person, place, or thing.

boy, city, frog

A **pronoun** takes the place of a noun.

he, it, they

An **adjective** describes a noun or a pronoun.

The (blue) frog had a (loud) croak.

Circle the adjectives in the sentences.

1. Colorful birds live in the bushy treetops.

2. The rainforest has different layers.

3. A big canopy forms a shady umbrella over the rainforest.

4. The thick understory is filled with interesting animals.

5. The cool, dark forest floor is home to insects and snakes.

6. Scarlet macaws are pretty rainforest birds.

7. Loud screams echoed through the dense forest.

8. Long green pythons can grow to be more than 300 pounds!

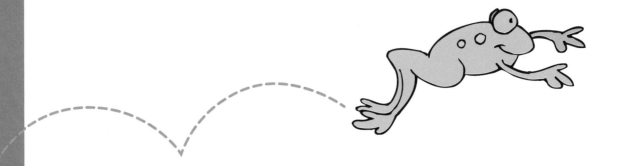

Spellamadoodle

Write each spelling word on the outline of the drawing. You may use each word more than once. For fun, decorate the drawing.

few	blue	clue	choose
ooze	dangerous	gentle	strange
giant	poison	cousin	toxic

Frog Fantasy

You are an explorer hiking in the rainforest. All of a sudden, you hear singing. When you turn, you see a small blue poison dart frog sitting on a branch. It's singing! And better yet, it can talk! Write a creative story about your conversation. What does the frog tell you? Use as many spelling words as you can.

few	blue	clue	choose
ooze	dangerous	gentle	strange
giant	poison	cousin	toxic

_____

_____

_____

_____

_____

_____

_____

_____

_____

✔ Edit Your Work

- ◯ I used complete sentences.
- ◯ I used correct spelling.
- ◯ I used correct capitalization and punctuation.

Creative Sentences

Skills:

Writing
Complete
Sentences

Using
Adjectives

Rewrite each sentence by adding adjectives that describe the underlined words.

1. The <u>jaguar</u> looked at me with its <u>eyes</u>.

_____

_____

2. <u>Squirrel monkeys</u> swing from the <u>trees</u>.

_____

_____

3. <u>Frogs</u> fill the floor of the <u>forest</u>.

_____

_____

4. That <u>snake</u> is slithering along the <u>river</u>.

_____

_____

5. The <u>frog</u> can attach itself to <u>leaves</u> and <u>trees</u>.

_____

_____

_____

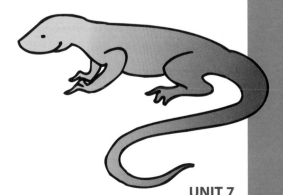

TEST YOUR SKILLS — Rainforest Frogs

Spelling Test

Find the correct answer. Fill in the circle.

1. Which word is an adjective?
   - ○ snake
   - ○ form
   - ○ blue

2. Which sentence contains an adjective?
   - ○ Birds live in trees.
   - ○ Babies cry.
   - ○ Green frogs croak.

3. Which word is spelled correctly?
   - ○ toksic
   - ○ poison
   - ○ couzin

4. Which word means "to flow out slowly"?
   - ○ ooze
   - ○ choose
   - ○ clue

Ask someone to test you on the spelling words.

1. _____
2. _____
3. _____
4. _____
5. _____
6. _____
7. _____
8. _____
9. _____
10. _____
11. _____
12. _____

5. Write the sentence correctly.

giante trees are a gentil cover for strang and dangerious rainforest animals

_____

_____

Spell & Write • EMC 4540 • © Evan-Moor Corporation

Animals in Space

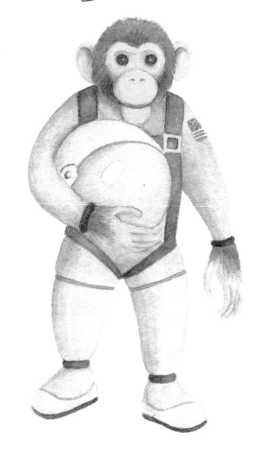

Humans have always dreamed of space travel. But animals were there first.

It was the early 1950s when the first animals made a successful trip into space. Eleven mice and a monkey rode the United States Aerobee rocket. The rocket went straight up and then down again. All the animals came back alive and well. But the first real space traveler was Laika, a Russian dog. In 1957, she took a trip on the Soviet spacecraft *Sputnik 2*. Her voyage amounted to ten long days. Her capsule traveled around the Earth. Sadly, Laika died during the flight. But she became a bright star in the Russian space program!

Next came Able and Baker, two squirrel monkeys. In 1959, they rode the American Jupiter C rocket. But the most famous monkey to fly in space was a chimp named Ham. In 1961, Ham began to train for his flight. He enjoyed learning. He learned to pull levers when he saw lights flash.
When he did his job right, he got a banana pellet! Ham's flight went as planned. But his capsule almost sank when it landed in the ocean! He might have drowned! Luckily, Ham was pulled to safety. Ham's voyage paved the way for human space travel.

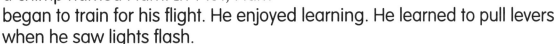

Find It! Read the spelling words.
Check off the words you can find in the story.

✓ flight	✓ bright	✓ might	✓ light
✓ drown	✓ amount	✓ around	✓ enjoy
✓ voyage	✓ famous	✓ rocket	✓ ocean

How many spelling words did you find? _____

Spelling Practice

Read and Spell

Copy and Spell

Spell It Again!

1. flight

2. bright

3. might

4. light

5. drown

6. amount

7. around

8. enjoy

9. voyage

10. famous

11. rocket

12. ocean

Search and Spell

Circle the word in each row that is spelled correctly.

1. light   lite   lighte
2. arownd   arond   around
3. droun   drown   ddrown
4. ocine   ocean   oshean
5. voiyag   voyage   voyege
6. bright   brigt   brite
7. amont   amownt   amount
8. enjoie   enjoy   injoy
9. mite   mihte   might
10. famous   fameus   famose
11. flyte   flight   fliyt
12. roket   rocket   rockite

Write a sentence using the spelling words *rocket* and *flight*.

_____

_____

Write a sentence using the spelling words *enjoy* and *voyage*.

_____

_____

Which Word?

Fill in each blank with the correct word.

1. I _____ want to ride a _____ to the moon.

rocket	famous	ocean	might

2. Ham was a _____ chimp who took a _____ into space.

light	enjoy	flight	famous

3. Do you _____ swimming in the _____?

enjoy	light	ocean	voyage

4. Laika's space _____ made her a _____ star.

amount	voyage	bright	might

5. That _____ has a flashing red _____ on the top.

light	rocket	flight	around

6. Ham did not _____ when his capsule crashed into the _____.

amount	light	ocean	drown

Capital Review

Use a capital letter for:

- the first word of a sentence
- people's first and last names, and their titles
- the names of special places and things
- the word that names yourself—I
- days, months, and holidays

Rewrite each sentence using correct capital letters.

1. on monday, i gave a speech on animal heroes.

   _____

   _____

2. two of these heroes are ham the chimp and laika the dog.

   _____

   _____

3. the united states has a great space program.

   _____

   _____

4. shuttles take off from cape canaveral in florida.

   _____

   _____

5. american men landed on the moon in july 1964.

   _____

   _____

6. laika traveled on the spacecraft sputnik 2.

   _____

   _____

Animal Astronaut Cinquain

A **cinquain** is a five-line poem with a specific number of words.

Line 1: Write a one-word subject.

Line 2: Write two words that describe the subject.

Line 3: Write three action words about the subject.

Line 4: Write a four-word statement about the subject.

Line 5: Write one word that refers back to the subject.

Write a cinquain about an animal space traveler. Use at least two spelling words in the cinquain. Look back at the story to help you.

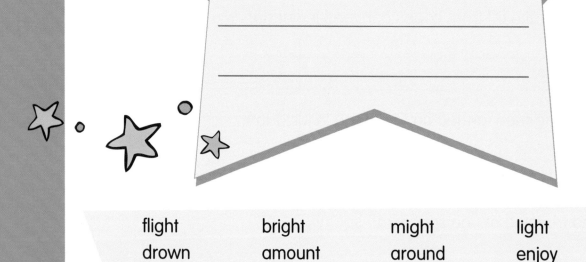

flight	bright	might	light
drown	amount	around	enjoy
voyage	famous	rocket	ocean

Spellamadoodle

Write each spelling word on the outline of the drawing. You may use the words more than once. For fun, decorate the drawing.

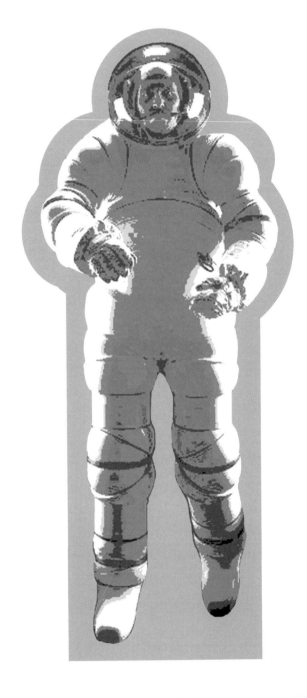

flight	bright	might	light
drown	amount	around	enjoy
voyage	famous	rocket	ocean

Time Capsule

3...2...1... Blastoff! Your rocket is racing through space.

You are on your way to Mars to drop off a time capsule. The capsule holds eight things that best describe you. What will you put in your time capsule? List your items below.

1. _____

_____

2. _____

_____

3. _____

_____

4. _____

_____

5. _____

_____

6. _____

_____

7. _____

_____

8. _____

_____

⭐ ⭐ ⭐

You Are Ham

Ham held the title of "First American Chimp in Space." Pretend you are Ham. Write a journal entry about one day on your spaceflight. What did you see through the window? What jobs were you trained to do? What did you do when your capsule landed in the ocean? Use as many spelling words as you can.

flight	bright	might	light
drown	amount	around	enjoy
voyage	famous	rocket	ocean

_____

_____

_____

_____

_____

_____

_____

_____

☆ ▢ ▢ ▢ ▭

✔ Edit Your Work

○ I used complete sentences.

○ I used correct spelling.

○ I used correct capitalization and punctuation.

Animals in Space

Spelling Test

Find the correct answer. Fill in the circle.

1. Which sentence has correct capitalization?
   - ◯ Laika and Ham are space heroes.
   - ◯ laika and ham are space heroes.
   - ◯ laika and Ham are space heroes.

2. Which sentence has correct capitalization?
   - ◯ james and i went to cape canaveral, Florida.
   - ◯ James and I went to cape canaveral, Florida.
   - ◯ James and I went to Cape Canaveral, Florida.

3. Which word is spelled correctly?
   - ◯ famous
   - ◯ famuss
   - ◯ famose

4. Which word means "to get pleasure from doing something"?
   - ◯ light
   - ◯ enjoy
   - ◯ bright

Ask someone to test you on the spelling words.

1. _____
2. _____
3. _____
4. _____
5. _____
6. _____
7. _____
8. _____
9. _____
10. _____
11. _____
12. _____

5. Write the sentence correctly.

   i migt engoy taking a voiyage through space on a roket

   _____

   _____

American Symbols

Most countries have special symbols. Two of America's symbols are the bald eagle and the Statue of Liberty.

When America was first formed, the founding fathers chose a bird to symbolize their new country. Many thought the bald eagle was a good choice. It was judged as the perfect symbol of freedom. On June 29, 1782, the bald eagle became America's symbol. It was chosen for its long life, great strength, and noble looks. Today, the bald eagle's image is captured on many American things, such as coins.

Another great symbol of freedom is the Statue of Liberty. France gave the statue to America in 1885 as a sign of friendship. French sculptor Frederic Bartholdi was hired to design it. It was supposed to be finished in 1876, but a lack of money put the project's completion in doubt. Lotteries, auctions, and even prizefights helped to raise more money. When the statue was finally brought to America, it was in 350 pieces! It had to be put back together. This great statue stands 152 feet tall. Even the index finger is 8 feet long!

Find It!

Read the spelling words.
Check off the words you can find in the story.

☐ thought	☐ ought	☐ brought	☐ caught
☐ auction	☐ design	☐ sign	☐ doubt
☐ judge	☐ symbol	☐ statue	☐ America

How many spelling words did you find? _____

Spelling Practice

Read and Spell	Copy and Spell	Spell It Again!
1. thought	_____	_____
2. ought	_____	_____
3. brought	_____	_____
4. caught	_____	_____
5. auction	_____	_____
6. design	_____	_____
7. sign	_____	_____
8. doubt	_____	_____
9. judge	_____	_____
10. symbol	_____	_____
11. statue	_____	_____
12. America	_____	_____

Circle and Spell

Circle the two misspelled words in each sentence. Write them correctly on the lines.

1. I thaut the bald eagle was a simbal of freedom.

   _____   _____

2. The Stachue of Liberty was given as a sine of friendship.

   _____   _____

3. I dout the desine will be finished by this week.

   _____   _____

4. The charity awction was cought on videotape.

   _____   _____

5. We ougt to judje these rules more carefully.

   _____   _____

6. She braught songs about Amarica to class.

   _____   _____

Fill in the missing letters for each spelling word.

1. ____ ____ ght   4. s ____ mb ____ l

2. d ____ ____ bt   5. st ____ t ____ e

3. ____ ____ ction   6. des ____ ____ n

Skills:

Matching
Words
with Their
Meanings

Spelling Words
with **ough**
and **au**

Silent Letters

Spelling
Theme
Vocabulary

Match the Meanings

Write the spelling word for each definition.

thought	ought	brought	caught
auction	design	sign	doubt
judge	symbol	statue	America

1. _____ an object that represents something else

2. _____ a model of something made from stone or metal

3. _____ to be uncertain

4. _____ a sale in which goods are sold to the person who bids the most money

5. _____ to have used your mind to form ideas

6. _____ to draw something that can be built or made

7. _____ to form an opinion

8. _____ to have taken something with you

Circle the silent letter in each spelling word below.

1. sign

2. judge

3. design

4. doubt

Poetry Time

Create an acrostic poem. Write a word or phrase that starts with each letter in the topic word. Use the words in the story to help you.

thought	ought	brought	caught
auction	design	sign	doubt
judge	symbol	statue	America

E _____

A _____

G _____

L _____

E _____

Dear Friend . . .

Use commas:

- to separate three or more words or phrases in a series
- to separate the day and year in a date
- to separate a city and state, province, or country
- after the greeting in a friendly letter
- after the closing in a friendly letter

Read the letter. Add commas where they are needed.

August 15 2004

Dear Brandon

My summer vacation has been great! My family finally got to New York New York two days ago. We saw lots of cars tall buildings and museums. We visited one museum filled with old paintings. We saw artwork by three famous artists named Monet Degas and O'Keeffe. We also saw art from Paris France and Florence Italy.

But today was my favorite day! We visited the Statue of Liberty. My sister brother and I counted 25 windows in her crown. We could see the whole city. We could even see across the river to Hoboken New Jersey! After a while, we came back down to have lunch. We had hamburgers salads fries and sodas. I can't wait to get home and tell you all about it!

Your friend

Maya

Spellamadoodle

Write each spelling word on the outline of the drawing. You may use each word more than once. For fun, decorate the drawing.

thought	ought	brought	caught
auction	design	sign	doubt
judge	symbol	statue	America

Skills:

Creative
Thinking

Using a
Graphic
Organizer

The Best American Bird

Can you think of another bird that would be a good symbol for America? Use this organizer to write your thoughts. Think of at least three qualities your bird has that make it a good symbol for America. Write them in the organizer.

Bird's Name: _____

For America

America has the Statue of Liberty and the Liberty Bell. It also has the flag and the bald eagle. What other symbol do you think would be good for America? It could be an object, animal, or something made up. Describe it below. Include your ideas about why it would be a good symbol. Use as many spelling words as you can.

thought	ought	brought	caught
auction	design	sign	doubt
judge	symbol	statue	America

My American symbol is: _____

It is called: _____

It stands for: _____

It looks like: _____

_____

_____

_____

This is a good symbol because: _____

_____

_____

_____

✓ Edit Your Work

○ I used complete sentences.

○ I used correct spelling.

○ I used correct capitalization and punctuation.

American Symbols

Spelling Test

Find the correct answer. Fill in the circle.

1. In which sentence are commas used correctly?

   ○ Dylan bought apples bananas, oranges and peaches.

   ○ Dylan bought, apples bananas, oranges, and peaches.

   ○ Dylan bought apples, bananas, oranges, and peaches.

2. In which sentence are commas used correctly?

   ○ Were you born on that cold, windy day on March 10, 1994?

   ○ Were you born on that cold windy day, on March, 10 1994?

   ○ Were you born on that cold, windy, day on March 10 1994?

3. Which word is spelled correctly?

   ○ Ammerica

   ○ Americah

   ○ America

4. Which word means "an object that represents something else"?

   ○ symbol

   ○ design

   ○ sign

Ask someone to test you on the spelling words.

1. _____

2. _____

3. _____

4. _____

5. _____

6. _____

7. _____

8. _____

9. _____

10. _____

11. _____

12. _____

5. Write the sentence correctly.

   well i thaugt the stachue of liberty was a simbal of freedom

   _____

   _____

Travel Diary

July 21, 2004

Today, my best friend Mateo and I flew to a tropical island! When we stepped off the plane, the fresh scent of sea salt was in the air. We walked along the beach. The sand was fine and white, like sugar. The sea was as clear and blue as a swimming pool. It's hard to express how beautiful it was.

A huge black volcano grabbed our attention. It loomed over the beach like a silent, stony giant. We made it our mission to climb all the way to the top. Mateo and I are great climbers. We've just never climbed a volcano before!

July 22, 2004

Well, we did it! Mateo and I climbed to the very top of the volcano. No expression could describe the view from up there. We could see all the way to the other side of the island. And we could see miles and miles of blue-green ocean! Mateo told me to be very quiet and listen. We heard the wind whistle in our ears. When we got back down to the beach, I lay in the warm sand and drank lemonade. What a great day!

Find It!

Read the spelling words.
Check off the words you can find in the story.

☐ island	☐ walked	☐ climber	☐ listen
☐ scent	☐ whistle	☐ express	☐ expression
☐ mission	☐ attention	☐ enough	☐ friend

How many spelling words did you find? _____

Spelling Practice

Read and Spell	Copy and Spell	Spell It Again!
1. island	_____	_____
2. walked	_____	_____
3. climber	_____	_____
4. listen	_____	_____
5. scent	_____	_____
6. whistle	_____	_____
7. express	_____	_____
8. expression	_____	_____
9. mission	_____	_____
10. attention	_____	_____
11. enough	_____	_____
12. friend	_____	_____

Crossword Challenge

Complete the crossword puzzle using the spelling words.

island	walked	climber	listen
scent	whistle	express	expression
mission	attention	enough	friend

Across

2. to pay attention so that you can hear something
3. as much as needed
4. an area surrounded by water
6. someone you know well and enjoy being with
7. to make a high, shrill sound by blowing air through your lips
9. a pleasant smell
12. to show what you feel or think by saying, doing, or writing something

Down

1. concentration and careful thought
5. a special job or task
8. a phrase that has a particular meaning
10. someone who climbs
11. moved on foot at an easy pace

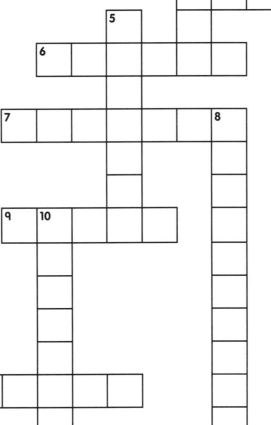

Skills:

Using
Sentence
Context to
Find Missing
Words

Silent Letters

Words in Context

Fill in the blanks with spelling words.

island	walked	climber	listen
scent	whistle	express	expression
mission	attention	enough	friend

1. I heard the faraway _____ of the train as I _____ home.

2. My best _____ and I visited a tropical _____.

3. The horn was loud _____ to grab my _____.

4. We stopped to _____ to the lovely music.

5. As an expert _____, my _____ is to climb this volcano.

6. "Just Do It" is an _____ most people know.

7. Journaling is a good way to _____ thoughts and feelings.

8. I smelled the fresh _____ of the ocean as I sat on the beach.

Circle the silent letter in each spelling word.

| scent | whistle | island |
| walked | listen | climber |

Word Search

Find and circle the spelling words. Words can go across, down, or diagonally.

island	walked	climber	listen
scent	whistle	express	expression
mission	attention	enough	friend

```
J  N  H  E  C  N  O  I  T  N  E  T  T  A  C
L  R  O  S  L  R  O  R  O  G  T  O  N  C  L
Y  I  T  N  I  T  B  I  S  L  A  N  D  Q  I
D  K  S  I  M  L  S  N  S  P  D  B  E  Q  L
G  Z  H  T  B  S  J  I  X  S  W  Q  U  C  N
O  A  M  F  E  I  Y  A  H  L  I  V  O  V  S
W  Y  B  R  R  N  W  M  F  W  H  M  M  Z  B
D  D  P  I  U  R  O  I  Q  E  A  X  P  X  K
O  X  C  E  O  H  A  U  D  B  C  L  J  K  D
E  E  K  N  Z  S  Z  U  G  A  Z  K  K  B  K
A  R  B  D  C  Y  H  Q  G  H  W  E  D  E  Z
S  H  B  P  U  F  E  X  P  R  E  S  S  B  D
```

Spellamadoodle

Write each spelling word on the outline of the drawing. You may use the words more than once. For fun, decorate the drawing.

island	walked	climber	listen
scent	whistle	express	expression
mission	attention	enough	friend

Quick Quotes

A **quotation** is the exact words a person says.

Quotation marks (" ") are placed before and after a speaker's exact words.

The first word inside the quotation marks begins with a capital letter.

"Next year, I want to visit China," Mom said.

Put quotation marks where they belong in each sentence. Be sure to use a capital letter for the first word inside the quotation marks.

1. Tana said Hawaii is my favorite island.

   _____

2. Mom said my favorite way to travel is by train.

   _____

3. I asked dad can I bring a friend to the movies?

   _____

4. Marco bragged I am the best climber in the class.

   _____

5. My teacher demanded class pay attention!

   _____

6. Lisa reminded listen to the train whistle.

   _____

Come and Visit!

Create a poster about the city or town where you live. This poster should make people want to visit your town. Tell about all the fun things to do there. Draw pictures to show what your town is like. Think of a fun title or caption that will grab visitors' attention.

island	walked	climber	listen
scent	whistle	express	expression
mission	attention	enough	friend

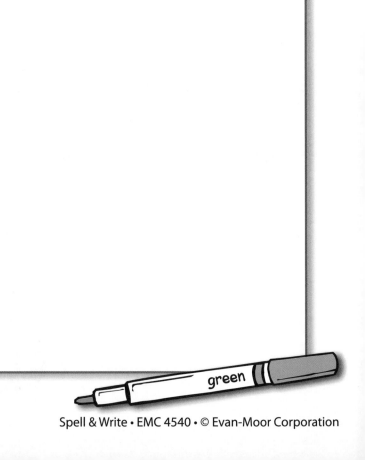

green

My Favorite Trip

Have you taken a special trip with friends or family? Where did you go? Who did you go with? How did you get there? What did you do? Describe your favorite part of the trip. Draw a picture in the frame below to show a "photo" from your trip.

_____

_____

_____

_____

_____

✔ **Edit Your Work**

◯ I used complete sentences.

◯ I used correct spelling.

◯ I used correct capitalization and punctuation.

Travel Diary

Spelling Test

Find the correct answer. Fill in the circle.

Ask someone to test you on the spelling words.

1. In which sentence are quotation marks used correctly?

   ○ "Mr. Lim told us, Study for the test on Friday."
   ○ Mr. Lim told us, "Study for the test on Friday.
   ○ Mr. Lim told us, "Study for the test on Friday."

2. In which sentence are quotation marks used correctly?

   ○ "I went to Mexico in June, Justin mentioned.
   ○ "I went to Mexico in June Justin mentioned."
   ○ "I went to Mexico in June," Justin mentioned.

3. Which word is spelled correctly?

   ○ expresion
   ○ expression
   ○ expressionn

4. Which word means "to pay attention so that you can hear something"?

   ○ listen
   ○ whistle
   ○ enough

1. _____

2. _____

3. _____

4. _____

5. _____

6. _____

7. _____

8. _____

9. _____

10. _____

11. _____

12. _____

5. Write the sentence correctly.

   i wocked around the illand with my freind, Kim said

   _____

   _____

Hero of the Sky

In 1932, Amelia Earhart was the first woman to fly solo across the Atlantic Ocean. After that, she wanted to be the first woman to fly around the world. She had already gained skill in flying through bad weather. She was awarded a U.S. Distinguished Flying Cross.

Amelia and her navigator departed from Oakland, California, and headed over the Pacific Ocean. They landed in New Guinea. The two had only 7,000 miles to go. They should have landed on Howland Island. They never made it there. People never heard from them again. Whether the plane crashed, no one knows. It remains a great mystery.

Nevertheless, Amelia Earhart lives on in history. She is a part of a league of daring women who did things that only men had done before.

Find It!

Read the spelling words.
Check off the words you can find in the story.

☐ two	☐ too	☐ their	☐ there
☐ weather	☐ great	☐ whether	☐ all ready
☐ already	☐ teacher	☐ league	☐ people

How many spelling words did you find? _____

Skills:

Homophones

Easily
Confused
Spellings

Sounds of **ea**

Spelling
Theme
Vocabulary

Visual Memory

Spelling Practice

Read and Spell	Copy and Spell	Spell It Again!
1. two	_____	_____
2. too	_____	_____
3. their	_____	_____
4. there	_____	_____
5. weather	_____	_____
6. whether	_____	_____
7. all ready	_____	_____
8. already	_____	_____
9. teacher	_____	_____
10. league	_____	_____
11. great	_____	_____
12. people	_____	_____

Crossword Challenge

Skills:

Matching Words with Their Meanings

Homophones

Easily Confused Spellings

Sounds of **ea**

Spelling Theme Vocabulary

Visual Memory

Complete the crossword puzzle using words from the spelling list. One word will not be used.

two	too	their	there
weather	great	whether	all ready
already	teacher	league	people

Across

2. that place
5. belonging to them
7. by this or that time
8. if
10. one who shows someone how to do something

Down

1. persons or human beings
2. the whole number that comes after 1 and before 3
3. a group of people with a common activity or interest
4. the condition of outside air at a certain time or place
6. very good or wonderful
9. as well

Skills:

Homophones

Easily Confused
Spellings

Sounds of **ea**

Spelling
Theme
Vocabulary

Using Context
Clues to Find
Missing Words

Auditory
Discrimination

Which Word?

Fill in each blank with the correct word or words.

1. We don't know _____ she is _____ for her trip.

   weather   whether   all ready   already

2. Did you see those _____ cats on the fence, _____?

   their   too   whether   two

3. _____ flight carried them all the way _____.

   there   their   already   teacher

4. Many _____ enjoy rainy _____.

   teacher   whether   people   weather

5. Our _____ has _____ given us lots of homework.

   all ready   already   people   teacher

Say each word aloud. What sound does ea make? Write each word under the correct heading.

| weather   all ready   great   teacher   league   already |

e as in bed	**e as in meet**	**a as in lake**
_____	_____	_____
_____	_____	_____

Tricky Titles

Titles of books, movies, plays, magazines, songs, stories, etc., are treated in specific ways.

- Capitalize the first word, the last word, and every important word in between.

Stories from the Blue Ocean

- When you write, underline the titles of books, movies, and television programs, and the names of newspapers and magazines.

Los Angeles Times (newspaper)   Rugrats (television show)

- Use quotation marks around the titles of stories, magazine articles, songs, and poems.

"The Star-Spangled Banner" (song)   "Little Boy Blue" (poem)

Rewrite each title. Use capital letters and correct punctuation.

1. somewhere over the rainbow _____

_____

2. the black stallion _____

3. the boston herald _____

4. ranger rick _____

5. mary had a little lamb _____

6. america the beautiful _____

7. finding nemo _____

8. sports illustrated for kids _____

_____

A Cinquain

A cinquain is a five-line poem with a specific number of words.

Line 1: Write a one-word subject.
Line 2: Write two words that describe the subject.
Line 3: Write three action words about the subject.
Line 4: Write a four-word statement about the subject.
Line 5: Write one word that refers back to the subject.

Create a cinquain about Amelia Earhart, another hero, or flight.

Spellamadoodle

Write each spelling word on the outline of the drawing. You may use the words more than once. For fun, decorate the drawing.

two	too	their	there
weather	great	whether	all ready
already	teacher	league	people

I Am a Hero!

Now, **you** are a hero! If you could do something great, what would it be? Would you write a novel? Run the fastest mile? Adopt a pet? Cure world hunger? Bring about world peace? Note your heroic deeds below on this medal. Use some of the spelling words.

two	too	their	there
weather	great	whether	all ready
already	teacher	league	people

So...What Was It Like?

You have the chance to go back in time! You have the opportunity to interview Amelia Earhart. What do you want to ask the missing pilot? Write six interview questions below.

✔ **Edit Your Work**

○ I used complete sentences.

○ I used correct spelling.

○ I used correct capitalization and punctuation.

Hero of the Sky

Spelling Test

Find the correct answer. Fill in the circle.

1. Which movie title has correct capitalization and punctuation?
   - ○ <u>The Fellowship of the Ring</u>
   - ○ "The Fellowship Of The Ring"
   - ○ The Fellowship of The ring

2. Which song title has correct capitalization and punctuation?
   - ○ "The Farmer In The Dell"
   - ○ "The Farmer in the Dell"
   - ○ The farmer in the dell

3. Which word is spelled correctly?
   - ○ leaghe
   - ○ leegue
   - ○ league

4. Which word means "that place"?
   - ○ there
   - ○ their
   - ○ whether

Ask someone to test you on the spelling words.

1. _____
2. _____
3. _____
4. _____
5. _____
6. _____
7. _____
8. _____
9. _____
10. _____
11. _____
12. _____

5. Write the sentence correctly.

   there too planes are already to fly 60 peepl all the way over their

   _____

   _____

Animal Helpers

Animals help people in many ways. Guide dogs are trained to help the blind navigate crowded buildings and city streets. But dogs, and even monkeys, are trained to happily perform many other tasks.

Hearing dogs are trained to alert their deaf handlers to important sounds. They know telephone rings, smoke alarms, and sirens. They can even recall the deaf person's name. The dog swiftly alerts the handler by pawing and then leading him or her to the sound.

Service animals, such as dogs and monkeys, help handlers who are confined to wheelchairs. The animals can pull the chairs, turn lights on and off, and open doors. They can also push elevator buttons and pick up or carry objects. Most of all, they help handlers rebuild their lives.

Some people in wheelchairs are unable to move their arms or legs. Capuchin monkeys are trained as helpers because their hands are like human hands. Monkeys can brush hair, serve food, and do housework. They can even help with CDs and videos! Service animals act as tireless friends. The special bond between animal and handler is unlike any other.

Find It!

Read the spelling words.
Check off the words you can find in the story.

happily	swiftly	hopeless	tireless
recall	rebuild	unable	unlike
service	alert	person	guide

How many spelling words did you find? _____

Skills:

Spelling Words with Suffixes –ly, –less

Prefixes un–, re–

R-Controlled Vowel (er)

Spelling Theme Vocabulary

Visual Memory

Spelling Practice

Read and Spell	Copy and Spell	Spell It Again!
1. happily	_____	_____
2. swiftly	_____	_____
3. hopeless	_____	_____
4. tireless	_____	_____
5. recall	_____	_____
6. rebuild	_____	_____
7. unable	_____	_____
8. unlike	_____	_____
9. service	_____	_____
10. alert	_____	_____
11. person	_____	_____
12. guide	_____	_____

Circle and Spell

Circle the word in each row that is spelled correctly.

1.	unabel	unable	inable
2.	sirvice	servis	service
3.	tirless	tirelis	tireless
4.	guide	gide	giude
5.	alirt	alert	alerte
6.	recall	reccalle	recale
7.	hapiley	happilly	happily
8.	unlicke	unlike	unlikk
9.	hopeless	hoples	hoplless
10.	swiftely	sweftly	swiftly
11.	pursen	person	pirsone
12.	rebuild	rebild	rebbuild

Skills:

Spelling Words with Suffixes **–ly**, **–less**

Prefixes **un–**, **re–**

R-Controlled Vowel (**er**)

Spelling Theme Vocabulary

Visual Memory

Skills:

Spelling Words with Suffixes **–ly, –less**

Prefixes **un–, re–**

R-Controlled Vowel (**er**)

Spelling Theme Vocabulary

Matching Words and Their Meanings

Match the Meanings

Write the spelling word for each definition.

happily	swiftly	hopeless	tireless
recall	rebuild	unable	unlike
service	alert	person	guide

1. _____ a human being

2. _____ in a cheerful or happy manner

3. _____ not able

4. _____ to build again

5. _____ a person or animal who shows the way

6. _____ not like

7. _____ without getting tired

8. _____ to remember something

9. _____ to warn or make someone aware of something

10. _____ the act or work of serving

11. _____ having or showing speed

12. _____ without hope

Clear the Confusion

Some words are easily confused. Take care to use the following words correctly:

Can/May

- Use can to tell that someone is able to do something.
    Maya can train guide dogs.

- Use may to ask or give permission to do something.
    May I watch you train the dogs?

Sit/Set

- Use sit to mean "stay seated."
    Sit down during the class.

- Use set to mean "to put or place."
    Please set the leash in the corner.

Use can, may, sit, or set to complete each sentence.

1. _____ I watch the monkeys play?

2. This service dog _____ carry a large backpack.

3. You may _____ here during the training film.

4. Hearing dogs _____ recall a person's name.

5. Watch the monkey _____ the plate on the table.

6. The monkeys _____ not climb on the furniture.

7. Did you teach these dogs to _____?

8. Some monkeys _____ brush people's hair and serve food.

9. This dog got the newspaper and _____ it on the porch.

10. _____ we take these service dogs out for a walk?

Word Search

Find and circle the spelling words. Words can go across, down, or diagonally.

```
Y  E  S  S  O  U  L  U  M  P
B  R  O  W  U  N  L  I  K  E
Y  O  E  V  E  A  A  B  L  E
L  L  D  A  U  B  C  A  L  L
T  T  I  R  E  L  E  S  S  T
F  R  U  P  O  E  R  Y  E  L
I  E  G  A  P  T  O  A  R  M
W  L  O  H  I  A  B  L  V  O
S  A  L  E  B  R  H  O  I  T
R  E  B  U  I  L  D  L  C  H
A  N  O  S  R  E  P  L  E  D
H  O  P  E  L  E  S  S  I  X
```

happily	swiftly	hopeless	tireless
recall	rebuild	unable	unlike
service	alert	person	guide

Spellamadoodle

Write each spelling word on the outline of the drawing. You may use the words more than once. For fun, decorate the drawing.

happily	swiftly	hopeless	tireless
recall	rebuild	unable	unlike
service	alert	person	guide

Helping Paws

You've read about the different ways animals help people. What other ways could animals help people? How could they help with sports or hobbies? Could they help at school? Write a list below. Be sure to write the kind of animal next to the task.

1. _____

_____

2. _____

_____

3. _____

_____

4. _____

_____

5. _____

_____

6. _____

_____

✔ **Edit Your Work**

◯ I used correct spelling.

◯ I used correct capitalization and punctuation.

Animal Friends

Do you know of or own a special animal? How does it help you or
its owner? How is this animal a good friend to you or someone
else? Write an acrostic poem about this animal. Begin each word,
phrase, or sentence with a letter in the topic word.

F _____

R _____

I _____

E _____

N _____

D _____

Find the correct answer. Fill in the circle.

Ask someone to test you on the spelling words.

1. Which sentence uses *can* or *may* correctly?

    ○ Can this dog identify the sound of a siren?

    ○ This dog may identify many different sounds.

    ○ Some people in wheelchairs may not be able to move their arms or legs.

2. Which sentence uses *sit* or *set* correctly?

    ○ Binky can sit out food on the dinner table.

    ○ The monkey likes to set on your lap.

    ○ Binky will sit in the chair until you call her.

3. Which word is spelled correctly?

    ○ guide

    ○ gide

    ○ giude

4. Which word means "to warn or make someone aware of something"?

    ○ person

    ○ recall

    ○ alert

1. _____

2. _____

3. _____

4. _____

5. _____

6. _____

7. _____

8. _____

9. _____

10. _____

11. _____

12. _____

5. Write the sentence correctly.

    sirvice animals hapilly help people who want to rebild their lives

    _____

    _____

Test Your Skills–Record Form

Unit	Test Page	Topic	Test Your Skills Score (5 possible)	Spelling Test Score (12 possible)
1	12	**Wild Winds**		
2	22	**Comets**		
3	32	**The Greeks Were First**		
4	42	**Unusual Pets**		
5	52	**They Changed the World**		
6	62	**The Buried City: Pompeii**		
7	72	**Rainforest Frogs**		
8	82	**Animals in Space**		
9	92	**American Symbols**		
10	102	**Travel Diary**		
11	112	**Hero of the Sky**		
12	122	**Animal Helpers**		

Pull-out Spelling Lists

Use these lists to give spelling tests, post on the refrigerator, and for extra practice.

Unit 1 Wild Winds	Unit 2 Comets	Unit 3 The Greeks Were First
1. believe	1. collide	1. ancient
2. people	2. million	2. oath
3. lightning	3. matter	3. heroes
4. explode	4. across	4. swore
5. freight	5. follow	5. brother
6. piece	6. litter	6. holiday
7. weigh	7. future	7. athlete
8. damage	8. usual	8. mountain
9. which	9. used	9. month
10. violent	10. beautiful	10. July
11. tornado	11. year	11. August
12. fact	12. cause	12. summer

Pull-out Spelling Lists

Use these lists to give spelling tests, post on the refrigerator, and for extra practice.

Unit 4 Unusual Pets	Unit 5 They Changed the World	Unit 6 The Buried City: Pompeii
1. they're	1. lived	1. also
2. don't	2. living	2. almost
3. couldn't	3. traveled	3. awful
4. aren't	4. traveling	4. awesome
5. who's	5. changed	5. early
6. everything	6. changing	6. earth
7. everyone	7. earlier	7. wonder
8. anyone	8. earliest	8. shower
9. anything	9. quicker	9. world
10. through	10. quickest	10. worst
11. curious	11. telephone	11. volcano
12. temperature	12. light	12. erupt

Pull-out Spelling Lists

Use these lists to give spelling tests, post on the refrigerator, and for extra practice.

Unit 7 Rainforest Frogs	Unit 8 Animals in Space	Unit 9 American Symbols
1. few	1. flight	1. thought
2. blue	2. bright	2. ought
3. clue	3. might	3. brought
4. choose	4. light	4. caught
5. ooze	5. drown	5. auction
6. dangerous	6. amount	6. design
7. gentle	7. around	7. sign
8. strange	8. enjoy	8. doubt
9. giant	9. voyage	9. judge
10. poison	10. famous	10. symbol
11. cousin	11. rocket	11. statue
12. toxic	12. ocean	12. America

Pull-out Spelling Lists

Use these lists to give spelling tests, post on the refrigerator, and for extra practice.

Unit 10 Travel Diary	Unit 11 Hero of the Sky	Unit 12 Animal Helpers
1. island	1. two	1. happily
2. walked	2. too	2. swiftly
3. climber	3. their	3. hopeless
4. listen	4. there	4. tireless
5. scent	5. weather	5. recall
6. whistle	6. whether	6. rebuild
7. express	7. all ready	7. unable
8. expression	8. already	8. unlike
9. mission	9. teacher	9. service
10. attention	10. league	10. alert
11. enough	11. great	11. person
12. friend	12. people	12. guide

Answer Key

Page 3

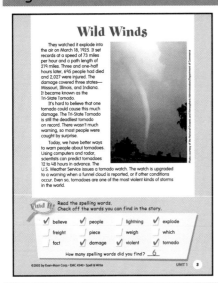

Page 5

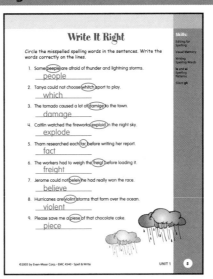

Page 6

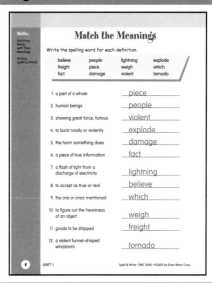

Page 7

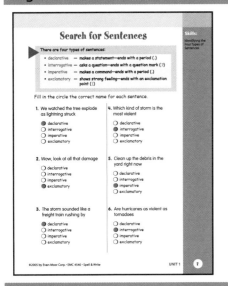

Page 8

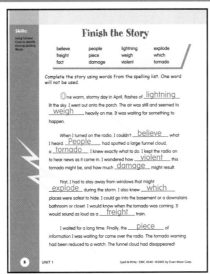

Page 10

Page 11

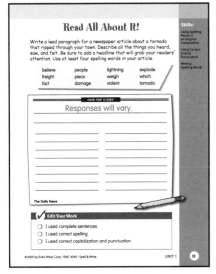

Page 12

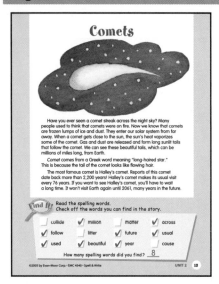

Comets

Have you ever seen a comet streak across the night sky? Many people used to think that comets were on fire. Now we know that comets are frozen lumps of ice and dust. They enter our solar system from far away. When a comet gets close to the sun, the sun's heat vaporizes some of the comet. Gas and dust are released and form sunlit tails that follow the comet. We can see these beautiful tails, which can be millions of miles long, from Earth.

Comet comes from a Greek word meaning "long-haired star." This is because the tail of the comet looks like flowing hair.

The most famous comet is Halley's comet. Reports of this comet date back more than 2,200 years! Halley's comet makes its usual visit every 76 years. If you want to see Halley's comet, you'll have to wait a long time. It won't visit Earth again until 2061, many years in the future.

Find It! Read the spelling words. Check off the words you can find in the story.

☐ collide	✓ million	☐ matter	✓ across
✓ follow	☐ litter	✓ future	✓ usual
✓ used	☐ beautiful	✓ year	☐ cause

How many spelling words did you find? **8**

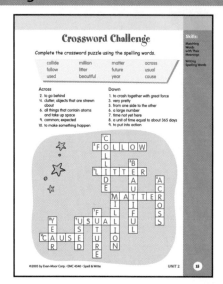

Crossword Challenge

Complete the crossword puzzle using the spelling words.

collide	million	matter	across
follow	litter	future	usual
used	beautiful	year	cause

Across
2. to go behind
4. clutter; objects that are strewn about
6. all things that contain atoms and take up space
9. common; expected
10. to make something happen

Down
1. to crash together with great force
3. very pretty
5. from one side to the other
6. a large number
7. time not yet here
8. a unit of time equal to about 365 days
9. to put into action

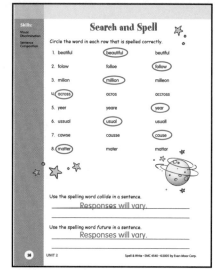

Search and Spell

Circle the word in each row that is spelled correctly.

1. beatiful — (beautiful) — beutiful
2. folow — folloe — (follow)
3. milion — (million) — milleon
4. (across) — acros — accross
5. yeer — yeare — (year)
6. ussual — (usual) — usuall
7. cawse — causse — (cause)
8. (matter) — mater — mattar

Use the spelling word *collide* in a sentence.
Responses will vary.

Use the spelling word *future* in a sentence.
Responses will vary.

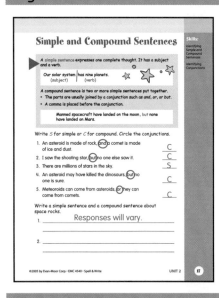

Simple and Compound Sentences

A simple sentence expresses one complete thought. It has a subject and a verb.

Our solar system has nine planets.
(subject) (verb)

A compound sentence is two or more simple sentences put together.
• The parts are usually joined by a conjunction such as and, or, or but.
• A comma is placed before the conjunction.

Manned spacecraft have landed on the moon, but none have landed on Mars.

Write *S* for simple or *C* for compound. Circle the conjunctions.

1. An asteroid is made of rock, and a comet is made of ice and dust. — **C**
2. I saw the shooting star, but no one else saw it. — **C**
3. There are millions of stars in the sky. — **S**
4. An asteroid may have killed the dinosaurs, but no one is sure. — **C**
5. Meteoroids can come from asteroids, or they can come from comets. — **C**

Write a simple sentence and a compound sentence about space rocks.

1. Responses will vary.

2.

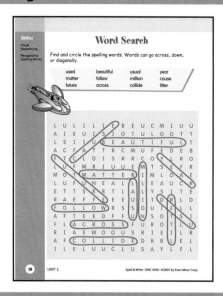

Word Search

Find and circle the spelling words. Words can go across, down, or diagonally.

used	beautiful	usual	year
matter	follow	million	cause
future	across	collide	litter

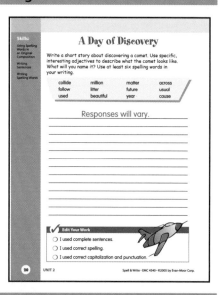

A Day of Discovery

Write a short story about discovering a comet. Use specific, interesting adjectives to describe what the comet looks like. What will you name it? Use at least six spelling words in your writing.

collide	million	matter	across
follow	litter	future	usual
used	beautiful	year	cause

Responses will vary.

✓ Edit Your Work
○ I used complete sentences.
○ I used correct spelling.
○ I used correct capitalization and punctuation.

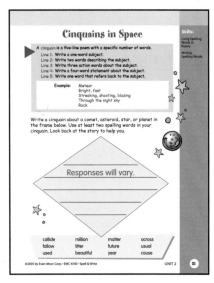

Cinquains in Space

A cinquain is a five-line poem with a specific number of words.
Line 1: Write a one-word subject.
Line 2: Write two words describing the subject.
Line 3: Write three action words about the subject.
Line 4: Write a four-word statement about the subject.
Line 5: Write one word that refers back to the subject.

Example: Meteor
Bright, fast
Streaking, shooting, blazing
Through the night sky
Rock

Write a cinquain about a comet, asteroid, star, or planet in the frame below. Use at least two spelling words in your cinquain. Look back at the story to help you.

Responses will vary.

collide	million	matter	across
follow	litter	future	usual
used	beautiful	year	cause

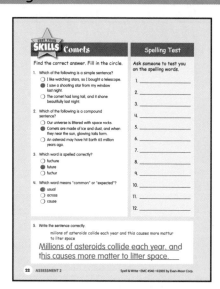

TEST YOUR SKILLS — Comets

Find the correct answer. Fill in the circle.

1. Which of the following is a simple sentence?
   ○ I like watching stars, so I bought a telescope.
   ● I saw a shooting star from my window last night.
   ○ The comet had long tail, and it shone beautifully last night.

2. Which of the following is a compound sentence?
   ○ Our universe is littered with space rocks.
   ● Comets are made of ice and dust, and when they near the sun, glowing tails form.
   ○ An asteroid may have hit Earth 65 million years ago.

3. Which word is spelled correctly?
   ○ fuchure
   ● future
   ○ fuchur

4. Which word means "common" or "expected"?
   ● usual
   ○ across
   ○ cause

5. Write the sentence correctly.
   millions of asteroids collide each year and this causes more mattur to litter space
   Millions of asteroids collide each year, and this causes more matter to litter space.

Spelling Test

Ask someone to test you on the spelling words.

1. _____
2. _____
3. _____
4. _____
5. _____
6. _____
7. _____
8. _____
9. _____
10. _____
11. _____
12. _____

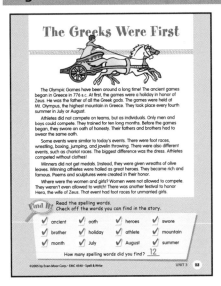

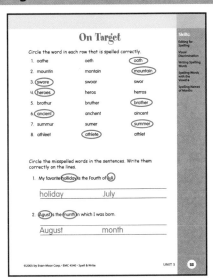

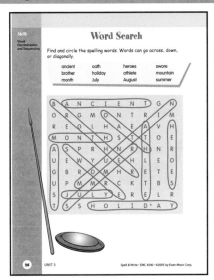

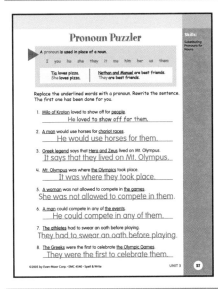

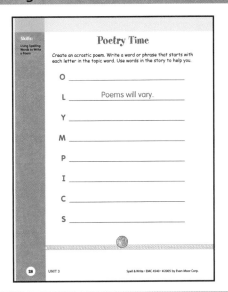

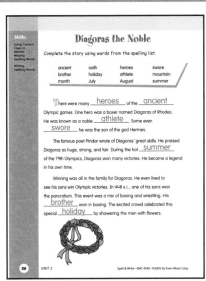

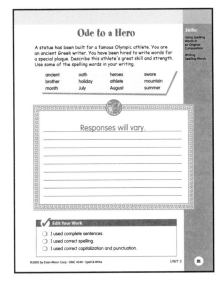

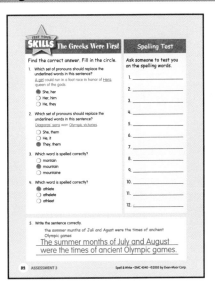

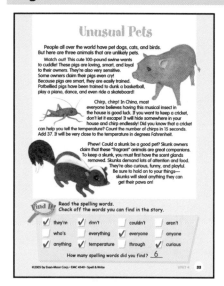

Unusual Pets

People all over the world have pet dogs, cats, and birds. But here are three animals that are unlikely pets.

Watch out! This cute 100-pound swine wants to cuddle! These pigs are loving, smart, and loyal to their owners. They're also very sensitive. Some owners claim their pigs even cry! Because pigs are smart, they are easily trained. Potbellied pigs have been trained to dunk a basketball, play a piano, dance, and even ride a skateboard!

Chirp, chirp! In China, most everyone believes having this musical insect in the house is good luck. If you want to keep a cricket, don't let it escape! It will hide somewhere in your house and chirp endlessly! Did you know that a cricket can help you tell the temperature? Count the number of chirps in 15 seconds. Add 37. It will be very close to the temperature in degrees Fahrenheit.

Phew! Could a skunk be a good pet? Skunk owners claim that these "fragrant" animals are great companions. To keep a skunk, you must first have the scent glands removed. Skunks demand lots of attention and food. They're also curious, funny, and playful. Be sure to hold on to your things—skunks will steal anything they can get their paws on!

Find it! Read the spelling words. Check off the words you can find in the story.

☑ they're   ☑ don't   ☐ couldn't   ☐ aren't
☐ who's   ☑ everything   ☑ everyone   ☐ anyone
☑ anything   ☑ temperature   ☐ through   ☑ curious

How many spelling words did you find? __6__

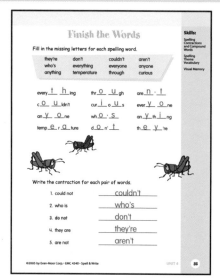

Finish the Words

Fill in the missing letters for each spelling word.

they're	don't	couldn't	aren't
who's	everything	everyone	anyone
anything	temperature	through	curious

every_t_ _h_ing   thr_o_ _u_ gh   are _n_ · _t_

c_o_ _u_ ldn't   cur_i_ _o_ _u_ s   any_v_ _o_ ne

an_y_ _o_ ne   wh_o_ · _s_   an_y_ th_i_ ng

temp_e_ _r_ a ture   d_o_ n · _t_   th_e_ _y_ 're

Write the contraction for each pair of words.

1. could not   _couldn't_
2. who is   _who's_
3. do not   _don't_
4. they are   _they're_
5. are not   _aren't_

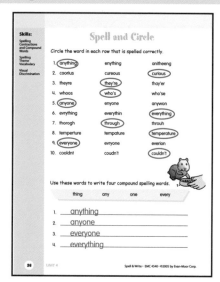

Spell and Circle

Circle the word in each row that is spelled correctly.

1. (anything)   enything   anitheeng
2. coorius   cureous   (curious)
3. theyre   (they're)   thay'er
4. whoos   (who's)   who'se
5. (anyone)   enyone   anywon
6. everything   everythin   (everything)
7. thorogh   (through)   throuh
8. temperture   tempature   (temperature)
9. (everyone)   everyone   everion
10. cooldnt   couldn't   (couldn't)

Use these words to write four compound spelling words.

| thing | any | one | every |

1. _anything_
2. _anyone_
3. _everyone_
4. _everything_

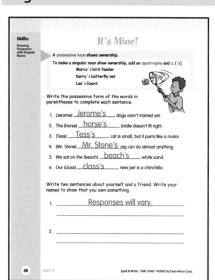

It's Mine!

A possessive noun shows ownership.

To make a singular noun show ownership, add an apostrophe and s. ('s)
Marco's bird feeder
Kerry's butterfly net
Les's lizard

Write the possessive form of the words in parentheses to complete each sentence.

1. (Jerome) _Jerome's_ dogs aren't trained yet.
2. The (horse) _horse's_ bridle doesn't fit right.
3. (Tess) _Tess's_ cat is small, but it purrs like a motor.
4. (Mr. Stone) _Mr. Stone's_ pig can do almost anything.
5. We sat on the (beach) _beach's_ white sand.
6. Our (class) _class's_ new pet is a chinchilla.

Write two sentences about yourself and a friend. Write your names to show that you own something.

1. _Responses will vary._

2. _____

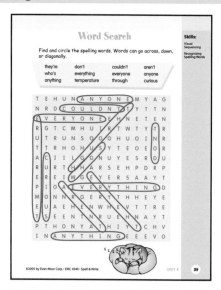

Word Search

Find and circle the spelling words. Words can go across, down, or diagonally.

they're	don't	couldn't	aren't
who's	everything	everyone	anyone
anything	temperature	through	curious

T E H U N A N Y O N E M Y A G
N R D C O U L D N T T Y T T N
E V E R Y O N E E H N E T E N
R G T C M H U I R T W T Y T R
U T R U N S O O O H U O I N R
T R H O H U S Y T E O E O R U
A C I I L G O N U Y E S R D U
R U R T H A R S E H P D R P
E R E I W G E Y E R S A A Y T
P I O A E V E R Y T H I N G O
M O N N R G E R Y T H H E Y E
E U A E H E N W H E V T T R E
T S E E N T N R U E H N A Y T
P T H O N Y A T H I Y T C H V
I N A N Y T H I N G E E E V O

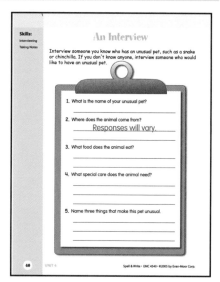

An Interview

Interview someone you know who has an unusual pet, such as a snake or chinchilla. If you don't know anyone, interview someone who would like to have an unusual pet.

1. What is the name of your unusual pet?
   _____

2. Where does the animal come from?
   Responses will vary.

3. What food does the animal eat?
   _____

4. What special care does the animal need?
   _____

5. Name three things that make this pet unusual.
   _____

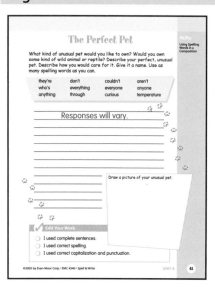

The Perfect Pet

What kind of unusual pet would you like to own? Would you own some kind of wild animal or reptile? Describe your perfect, unusual pet. Describe how you would care for it. Give it a name. Use as many spelling words as you can.

they're	don't	couldn't	aren't
who's	everything	everyone	anyone
anything	through	curious	temperature

Responses will vary.

Draw a picture of your unusual pet.

Edit Your Work
☐ I used complete sentences.
☐ I used correct spelling.
☐ I used correct capitalization and punctuation.

TEST YOUR SKILLS   **Unusual Pets**   **Spelling Test**

Find the correct answer. Fill in the circle.   Ask someone to test you on the spelling words.

1. Which word shows possession correctly?
   ○ Jamies' baseball
   ○ Mia's tarantula
   ● the woman's coat

2. Which word shows possession correctly?
   ● our family's pets
   ○ the pigs ears
   ○ the skunk's tail

3. Which word is spelled correctly?
   ○ tempature
   ● temperature
   ○ temperture

4. Which word means "eager to find out"?
   ○ cannibal
   ○ couldn't
   ● curious

1. _____
2. _____
3. _____
4. _____
5. _____
6. _____
7. _____
8. _____
9. _____
10. _____
11. _____
12. _____

5. Write the sentence correctly.
   they'er curios about snakes, but they dont know anething about feeding them

   They're curious about snakes, but they
   don't know anything about feeding them.

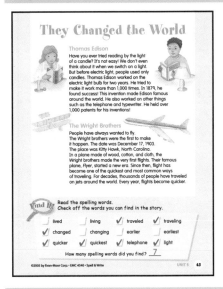

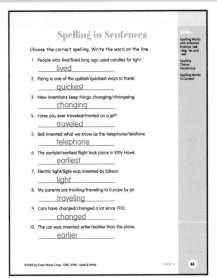

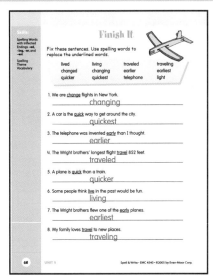

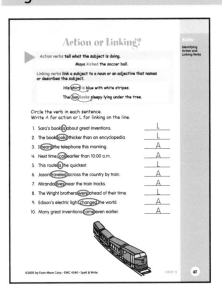

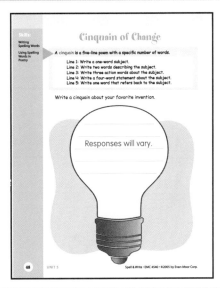

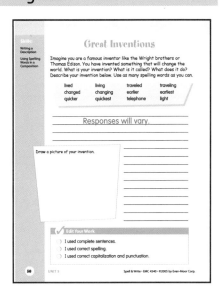

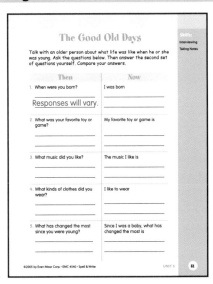

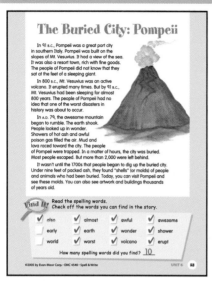

The Buried City: Pompeii

In 91 B.C., Pompeii was a great port city in southern Italy. Pompeii was built on the slopes of Mt. Vesuvius. It had a view of the sea. It was also a resort town, rich with fine goods. The people of Pompeii did not know that they sat at the feet of a sleeping giant.

In 800 B.C., Mt. Vesuvius was an active volcano. It erupted many times. But by 91 B.C., Mt. Vesuvius had been sleeping for almost 800 years. The people of Pompeii had no idea that one of the worst disasters in history was about to occur.

In A.D. 79, the awesome mountain began to rumble. The earth shook. People looked up in wonder. Showers of hot ash and awful poison gas filled the air. Mud and lava raced toward the city. The people of Pompeii were trapped. In a matter of hours, the city was buried. Most people escaped. But more than 2,000 were left behind.

It wasn't until the 1700s that people began to dig up the buried city. Under nine feet of packed ash, they found "shells" (or molds) of people and animals who had been buried. Today, you can visit Pompeii and see these molds. You can also see artwork and buildings thousands of years old.

Find It! Read the spelling words. Check off the words you can find in the story.

☑ also ☑ almost ☑ awful ☑ awesome
☐ early ☑ earth ☑ wonder ☑ shower
☐ world ☑ worst ☑ volcano ☑ erupt

How many spelling words did you find? __10__

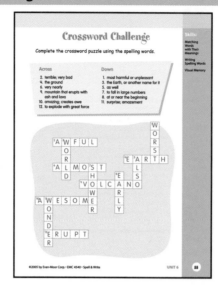

Crossword Challenge

Complete the crossword puzzle using the spelling words.

Skills:
Matching Words with Their Meanings
Writing Spelling Words
Visual Memory

Across
2. terrible; very bad
4. the ground
6. very nearly
9. mountain that erupts with ash and lava
10. amazing; creates awe
12. to explode with great force

Down
1. most harmful or unpleasant
3. the Earth, or another name for it
5. as well
7. to fall in large numbers
8. at or near the beginning
11. surprise; amazement

Crossword answers: WORST, AWFUL, WORD, EARTH, ALMOST, ELSE, VOLCANO, AWESOME, WONDER, ERUPT

Skills:
Visual Sequencing
Recognizing Spelling Words

Word Search

Find and circle the spelling words. Words can go across, down, or diagonally.

also almost awful awesome
early earth wonder shower
world worst volcano erupt

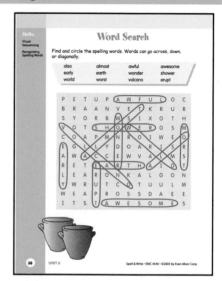

Present, Past, or Future?

Skills:
Identifying Present, Past, and Future Tense

The tense of a verb tells when an action occurs. Endings or helping verbs are added to change the tense.

- present—The action is happening now.
  Mina *talks* to her best friend.
- past—The action already happened.
  Mina *talked* to her best friend.
- future—The action is going to happen.
  Mina *will talk* to her best friend.

Circle the correct form of the verb.

1. The volcano erupted/(will erupt) in five days.
2. Even now, Jamie (climbs)/climbed volcanoes every summer.
3. Brad enjoys/(will enjoy) reading this volcano book tomorrow.
4. I (watched)/watch the eruption yesterday.
5. Tham constantly (researches)/will research Pompeii.
6. Ash and gas shower/(showered) into the air in 91 B.C.

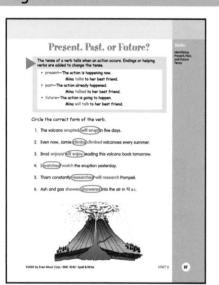

Poetry Time

Skills:
Using Spelling Words in a Poem

Create an acrostic poem. Write a word or phrase that starts with each letter in the topic word. Use the words in the story to help you.

V _____ Responses will vary.
O _____
L _____
C _____
A _____
N _____
O _____

Skills:
Using Context Clues to Identify Missing Spelling Words
Writing Spelling Words

Mount St. Helens

Complete the story using words from the spelling list. One word will not be used.

also almost awful awesome
early earth wonder shower
world worst volcano erupt

It was May 18, 1980, in Washington State. Something __awful__ was about to happen! __Early__ on this Sunday morning, Mount St. Helens sprang into action. No one thought this sleeping __volcano__ could __erupt__. First, the __earth__ shook with a large earthquake. Then, this __awesome__ volcano began spewing a __shower__ of ash and lava into the air. __Almost__ the entire north face of the mountain collapsed. This was the __worst__ eruption that had happened in years. Nearly 150 square miles of land was destroyed.

The volcano continues to erupt off and on. Now, this beautiful place is __also__ a national monument. You can visit the park. It's a __wonder__ to see!

This Is How It Happened

Skills:
Writing a Report
Writing Spelling Words
Giving an Oral Report

You are a TV reporter sent to report on the eruption of a volcano. This newly discovered volcano has been exploding for several hours. Describe what you see, hear, and smell. Use as many spelling words as you can. Then read your report aloud, as if you are on TV!

also almost awful awesome
early earth wonder shower
world worst volcano erupt

Responses will vary.

☑ **Edit Your Work**
○ I used complete sentences.
○ I used correct spelling.
○ I used correct capitalization and punctuation.

TEST YOUR SKILLS The Buried City: Pompeii **Spelling Test**

Find the correct answer. Fill in the circle.

1. Is the verb in this sentence present, past, or future tense?
   Ira travels the world to visit volcanoes.
   ● present
   ○ past
   ○ future

2. Is the verb in this sentence present, past, or future tense?
   Mai Le will write about the volcano's next eruption.
   ○ present
   ○ past
   ● future

3. Which word is spelled correctly?
   ○ wurst
   ○ whorst
   ● worst

4. Which word means "surprise" or "amazement"?
   ● wonder
   ○ shower
   ○ world

5. Write the sentence correctly.
   jake will tell us that the world's most awesome volcano will erupt soon
   Jake will tell us that the world's most awesome volcano will erupt soon.

Ask someone to test you on the spelling words.

1. _____
2. _____
3. _____
4. _____
5. _____
6. _____
7. _____
8. _____
9. _____
10. _____
11. _____
12. _____

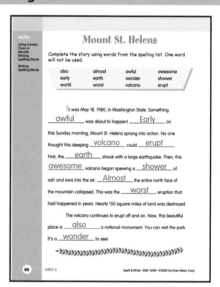
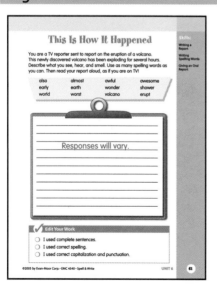
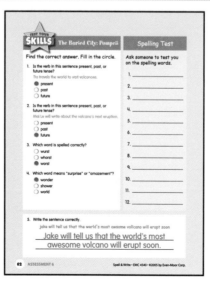

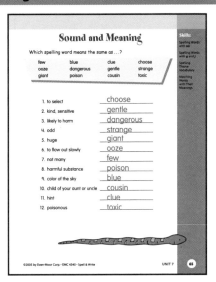

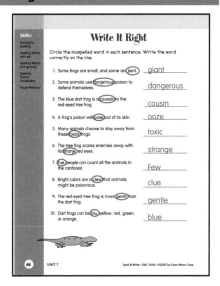

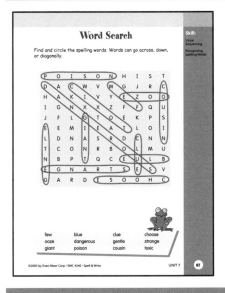

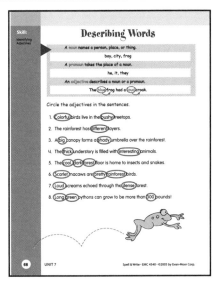

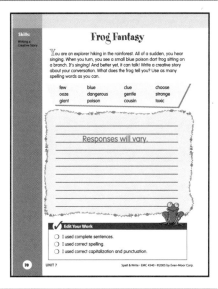

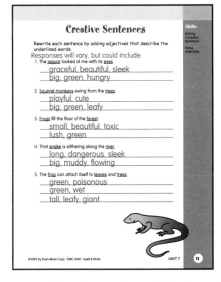

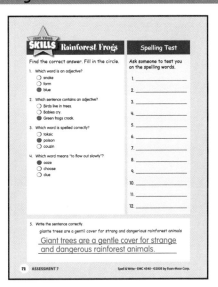

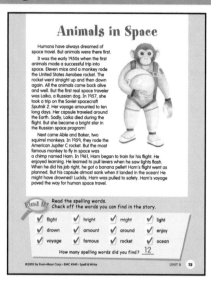

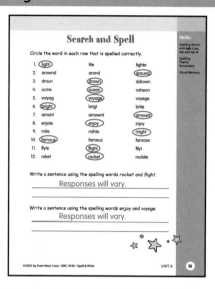

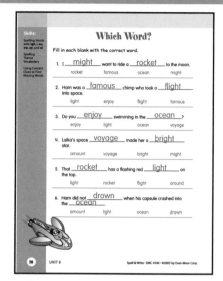

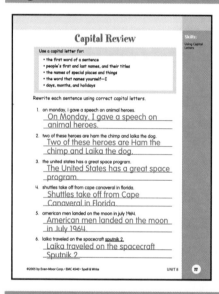

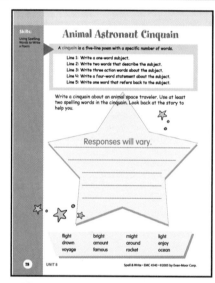

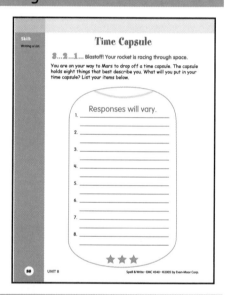

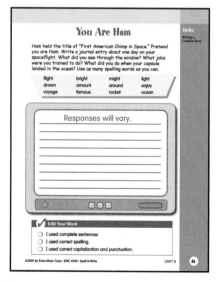

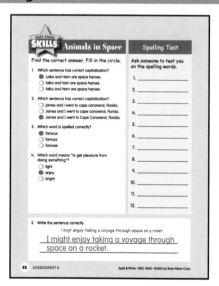

American Symbols

Most countries have special symbols. Two of America's symbols are the bald eagle and the Statue of Liberty.

When America was first formed, the founding fathers chose a bird to symbolize their new country. Many thought the bald eagle was a good choice. It was judged as the perfect symbol of freedom. On June 29, 1782, the bald eagle became America's symbol. It was chosen for its long life, great strength, and noble looks. Today, the bald eagle's image is captured on many American things, such as coins.

Another great symbol of freedom is the Statue of Liberty. France gave the statue to America in 1885 as a sign of friendship. French sculptor Frederic Bartholdi was hired to design it. It was supposed to be finished in 1876, but a lack of money put the project's completion in doubt. Lotteries, auctions, and even prizefights helped to raise more money. When the statue was finally brought to America, it was in 350 pieces! It had to be put back together. This great statue stands 152 feet tall. Even the index finger is 8 feet long!

Find It! Read the spelling words. Check off the words you can find in the story.

✓	thought	✓	ought	✓	brought		caught
✓	auction	✓	design	✓	sign	✓	doubt
✓	judge	✓	symbol	✓	statue	✓	America

How many spelling words did you find? **10**

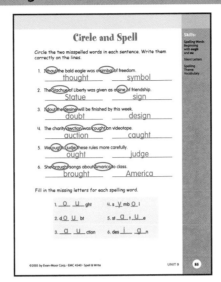

Circle and Spell

Circle the two misspelled words in each sentence. Write them correctly on the lines.

1. I thaught the bald eagle was a simbol of freedom.
   thought　　**symbol**

2. The Stachue of Liberty was given as a sine of friendship.
   Statue　　**sign**

3. I dout the desine will be finished by this week.
   doubt　　**design**

4. The charity awction was cought on videotape.
   auction　　**caught**

5. We ought to judje these rules more carefully.
   ought　　**judge**

6. She braught songs about Amereca to class.
   brought　　**America**

Fill in the missing letters for each spelling word.

1. _o_ _u_ ght
2. d _o_ _u_ bt
3. _a_ _u_ ction
4. s _y_ mb _o_ l
5. st _a_ _t_ _u_ e
6. des _i_ _g_ n

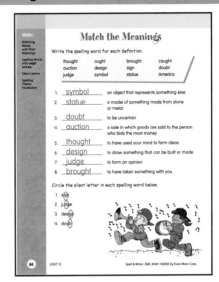

Match the Meanings

Write the spelling word for each definition.

thought	ought	brought	caught
auction	design	sign	doubt
judge	symbol	statue	America

1. **symbol** — an object that represents something else
2. **statue** — a model of something made from stone or metal
3. **doubt** — to be uncertain
4. **auction** — a sale in which goods are sold to the person who bids the most money
5. **thought** — to have used your mind to form ideas
6. **design** — to draw something that can be built or made
7. **judge** — to form an opinion
8. **brought** — to have taken something with you

Circle the silent letter in each spelling word below.

1. sign
2. judge
3. design
4. doubt

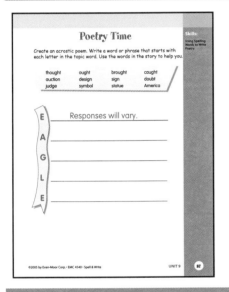

Poetry Time

Create an acrostic poem. Write a word or phrase that starts with each letter in the topic word. Use the words in the story to help you.

thought	ought	brought	caught
auction	design	sign	doubt
judge	symbol	statue	America

E
A
G　Responses will vary.
L
E

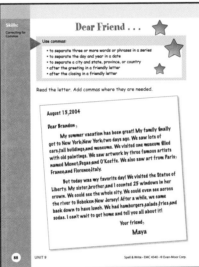

Dear Friend . . .

Use commas:
- to separate three or more words or phrases in a series
- to separate the day and year in a date
- to separate a city and state, province, or country
- after the greeting in a friendly letter
- after the closing in a friendly letter

Read the letter. Add commas where they are needed.

August 15, 2004

Dear Brandon,

My summer vacation has been great! My family finally got to New York, New York, two days ago. We saw lots of cars, tall buildings, and museums. We visited one museum filled with old paintings. We saw artwork by three famous artists named Monet, Degas, and O'Keeffe. We also saw art from Paris, France, and Florence, Italy.

But today was my favorite day! We visited the Statue of Liberty. My sister, brother, and I counted 25 windows in her crown. We could see the whole city. We could even see across the river to Hoboken, New Jersey! After a while, we came back down to have lunch. We had hamburgers, salads, fries, and sodas. I can't wait to get home and tell you all about it!

Your friend,
Maya

The Best American Bird

Can you think of another bird that would be a good symbol for America? Use this organizer to write your thoughts. Think of at least three qualities your bird has that make it a good symbol for America. Write them in the organizer.

Bird's Name: _____

Responses will vary.

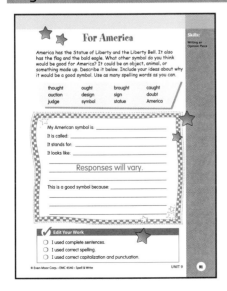

For America

America has the Statue of Liberty and the Liberty Bell. It also has the flag and the bald eagle. What other symbol do you think would be good for America? It could be an object, animal, or something made up. Describe it below. Include your ideas about why it would be a good symbol. Use as many spelling words as you can.

thought	ought	brought	caught
auction	design	sign	doubt
judge	symbol	statue	America

My American symbol is: _____
It is called: _____
It stands for: _____
It looks like: _____

Responses will vary.

This is a good symbol because: _____

Edit Your Work
- ○ I used complete sentences.
- ○ I used correct spelling.
- ○ I used correct capitalization and punctuation.

SKILLS American Symbols　　Spelling Test

Find the correct answer. Fill in the circle.

1. In which sentence are commas used correctly?
   - ○ Dylan bought apples bananas, oranges and peaches.
   - ○ Dylan bought, apples bananas, oranges, and peaches.
   - ● Dylan bought apples, bananas, oranges, and peaches.

2. In which sentence are commas used correctly?
   - ● Were you born on that cold, windy day on March 10, 1994?
   - ○ Were you born on that cold windy day, on March, 10 1994?
   - ○ Were you born on that cold, windy, day on March 10 1994?

3. Which word is spelled correctly?
   - ○ Ammerica
   - ○ Americh
   - ● America

4. Which word means "an object that represents something else"?
   - ● symbol
   - ○ design
   - ○ sign

5. Write the sentence correctly.
   well i thought the stachue of liberty was a simbal of freedom
   Well, I thought the Statue of Liberty was a symbol of freedom.

Ask someone to test you on the spelling words.

1. _____
2. _____
3. _____
4. _____
5. _____
6. _____
7. _____
8. _____
9. _____
10. _____
11. _____
12. _____

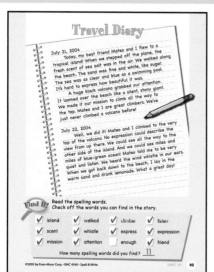

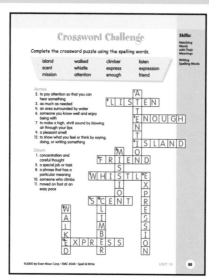

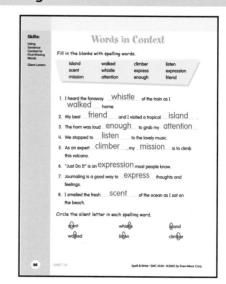

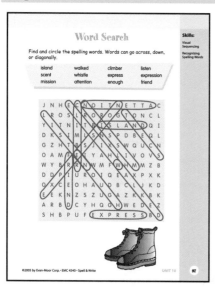

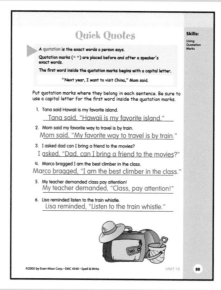

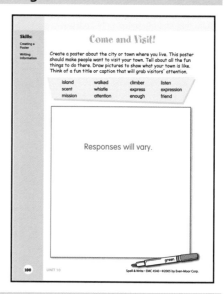

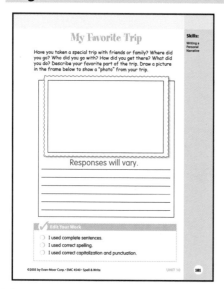

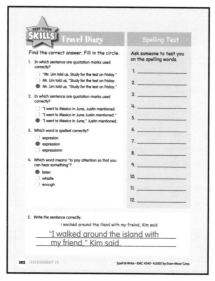

Spell & Write • EMC 4540 • © Evan-Moor Corporation

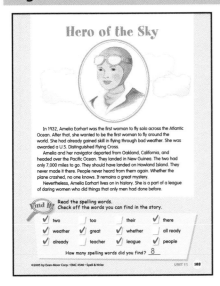

Page 103 — Hero of the Sky

In 1932, Amelia Earhart was the first woman to fly solo across the Atlantic Ocean. After that, she wanted to be the first woman to fly around the world. She had already gained skill in flying through bad weather. She was awarded a U.S. Distinguished Flying Cross.

Amelia and her navigator departed from Oakland, California, and headed over the Pacific Ocean. They landed in New Guinea. The two had only 7,000 miles to go. They should have landed on Howland Island. They never made it there. People never heard from them again. Whether the plane crashed, no one knows. It remains a great mystery.

Nevertheless, Amelia Earhart lives on in history. She is a part of a league of daring women who did things that only men had done before.

Find It! — Read the spelling words. Check off the words you can find in the story.

✓ two | ✓ too | ✓ their | ✓ there
✓ weather | ✓ great | ✓ whether | all ready
✓ already | teacher | league | people

How many spelling words did you find? 8

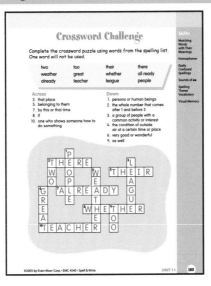

Page 105 — Crossword Challenge

Complete the crossword puzzle using words from the spelling list. One word will not be used.

two · weather · already · too · great · teacher · their · whether · league · there · all ready · people

Across
2. that place
5. belonging to them
7. by this or that time
8. if
10. one who shows someone how to do something

Down
1. persons or human beings
2. the whole number that comes after 1 and before 3
3. a group of people with a common activity or interest
4. the condition of outside air at a certain time or place
6. very good or wonderful
9. as well

Crossword answers: THERE, THEIR, ALREADY, WHETHER, TEACHER, POPLE/PEOPLE, WEATHER, LEAGUE, GREAT, TWO

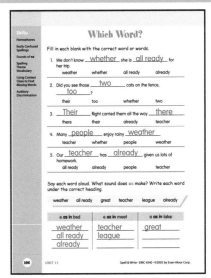

Page 106 — Which Word?

Fill in each blank with the correct word or words.

1. We don't know __whether__ she is __all ready__ for her trip.
   weather · whether · all ready · already

2. Did you see those __two__ cats on the fence, __too__?
   their · too · whether · two

3. __Their__ flight carried them all the way up __there__.
   there · their · already · teacher

4. Many __people__ enjoy rainy __weather__.
   teacher · whether · people · weather

5. Our __teacher__ has __already__ given us lots of homework.
   all ready · already · people · teacher

Say each word aloud. What sound does *ea* make? Write each word under the correct heading.

weather · all ready · great · teacher · league · already

e as in bed	e as in meet	a as in lake
weather	teacher	great
all ready	league	
already		

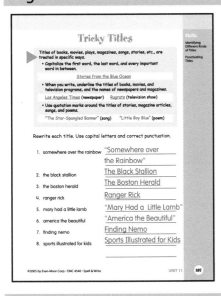

Page 107 — Tricky Titles

Titles of books, movies, plays, magazines, songs, stories, etc., are treated in specific ways.

• Capitalize the first word, the last word, and every important word in between.

Stories from the Blue Ocean

• When you write, underline the titles of books, movies, and television programs, and the names of newspapers and magazines.

Los Angeles Times (newspaper)   Rugrats (television show)

• Use quotation marks around the titles of stories, magazine articles, songs, and poems.

"The Star-Spangled Banner" (song)   "Little Boy Blue" (poem)

Rewrite each title. Use capital letters and correct punctuation.

1. somewhere over the rainbow — "Somewhere over the Rainbow"
2. the black stallion — The Black Stallion
3. the boston herald — The Boston Herald
4. ranger rick — Ranger Rick
5. mary had a little lamb — "Mary Had a Little Lamb"
6. america the beautiful — "America the Beautiful"
7. finding nemo — Finding Nemo
8. sports illustrated for kids — Sports Illustrated for Kids

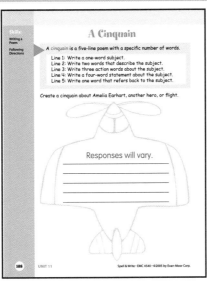

Page 108 — A Cinquain

A cinquain is a five-line poem with a specific number of words.

Line 1: Write a one-word subject.
Line 2: Write two words that describe the subject.
Line 3: Write three action words about the subject.
Line 4: Write a four-word statement about the subject.
Line 5: Write one word that refers back to the subject.

Create a cinquain about Amelia Earhart, another hero, or flight.

Responses will vary.

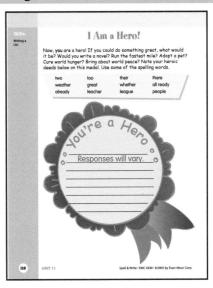

Page 110 — I Am a Hero!

Now, you are a hero! If you could do something great, what would it be? Would you write a novel? Run the fastest mile? Adopt a pet? Cure world hunger? Bring about world peace? Note your heroic deeds below on this medal. Use some of the spelling words.

two · weather · already · too · great · teacher · their · whether · league · there · all ready · people

You're a Hero

Responses will vary.

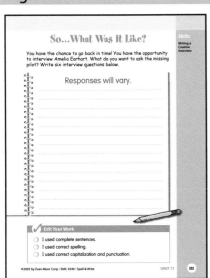

Page 111 — So...What Was It Like?

You have the chance to go back in time! You have the opportunity to interview Amelia Earhart. What do you want to ask the missing pilot? Write six interview questions below.

Responses will vary.

Edit Your Work
○ I used complete sentences.
○ I used correct spelling.
○ I used correct capitalization and punctuation.

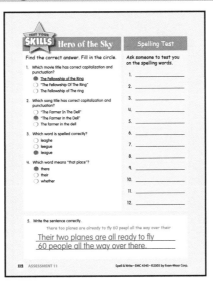

Page 112 — Hero of the Sky / Spelling Test

Find the correct answer. Fill in the circle.

1. Which movie title has correct capitalization and punctuation?
   ● "The Fellowship of the Ring"
   ○ "The Fellowship Of The Ring"
   ○ The Fellowship of The ring

2. Which song title has correct capitalization and punctuation?
   ○ "The Farmer In The Dell"
   ● "The Farmer in the Dell"
   ○ The farmer in the dell

3. Which word is spelled correctly?
   ○ leaghe
   ○ leegue
   ● league

4. Which word means "that place"?
   ● there
   ○ their
   ○ whether

5. Write the sentence correctly.
   there too planes are already to fly 60 peopl all the way over their
   Their two planes are all ready to fly 60 people all the way over there.

Ask someone to test you on the spelling words.
1. _____
2. _____
3. _____
4. _____
5. _____
6. _____
7. _____
8. _____
9. _____
10. _____
11. _____
12. _____

Animal Helpers

Animals help people in many ways. Guide dogs are trained to help the blind navigate crowded buildings and city streets. But dogs, and even monkeys, are trained to happily perform many other tasks.

Hearing dogs are trained to alert their deaf handlers to important sounds. They know telephone rings, smoke alarms, and sirens. They can even recall the deaf person's name. The dog swiftly alerts the handler by pawing and then leading him or her to the sound.

Service animals, such as dogs and monkeys, help handlers who are confined to wheelchairs. The animals can pull the chairs, turn lights on and off, and open doors. They can also push elevator buttons and pick up or carry objects. Most of all, they help handlers rebuild their lives.

Some people in wheelchairs are unable to move their arms or legs. Capuchin monkeys are trained as helpers because their hands are like human hands. Monkeys can brush hair, serve food, and do housework. They even help with CDs and videos! Service animals act as tireless friends. The special bond between animal and handler is unlike any other.

Find It! Read the spelling words. Check off the words you can find in the story.

✓ happily	✓ swiftly	hopeless	tireless
✓ recall	✓ rebuild	✓ unable	unlike
✓ service	✓ alert	person	✓ guide

How many spelling words did you find? 11

©2005 by Evan-Moor Corp. • EMC 4540 • Spell & Write — UNIT 12 — 113

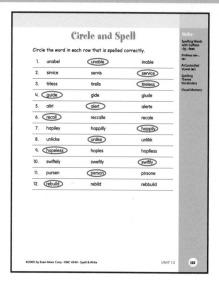

Circle and Spell

Skills: Spelling Words with Suffixes –ly, –less; Prefixes un–, re–; R-Controlled Vowel (er); Spelling Theme Vocabulary; Visual Memory

Circle the word in each row that is spelled correctly.

1. unabel — (unable) — inable
2. sirvice — servis — (service)
3. tireless — tirelis — (tireless)
4. (guide) — gide — giude
5. alirt — (alert) — alerte
6. (recall) — reccalle — recale
7. hapiley — happily — (happily)
8. unlicke — (unlike) — unlikk
9. (hopeless) — hoples — hopless
10. swiftely — swiftly — (swiftly)
11. pursen — (person) — pirsone
12. (rebuild) — rebild — rebbuild

©2005 by Evan-Moor Corp. • EMC 4540 • Spell & Write — UNIT 12 — 115

Skills: Spelling Words with Suffixes –ly, –less; Prefixes un–, re–; R-Controlled Vowel (er); Spelling Theme Vocabulary; Matching Words and Their Meanings

Match the Meanings

Write the spelling word for each definition.

happily	swiftly	hopeless	tireless
recall	rebuild	unable	unlike
service	alert	person	guide

1. person — a human being
2. happily — in a cheerful or happy manner
3. unable — not able
4. rebuild — to build again
5. guide — a person or animal who shows the way
6. unlike — not like
7. tireless — without getting tired
8. recall — to remember something
9. alert — to warn or make someone aware of something
10. service — the act or work of serving
11. swiftly — having or showing speed
12. hopeless — without hope

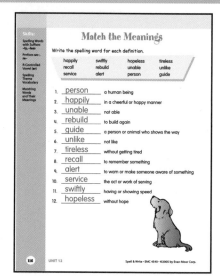

116 — UNIT 12 — Spell & Write • EMC 4540 • ©2005 by Evan-Moor Corp.

Clear the Confusion

Skills: Using Easily Confused Words can/ may, sit/set; Using Sentence Context to Find Missing Words

Some words are easily confused. Take care to use the following words correctly:

Can/May
• Use can to tell that someone is able to do something.
  Maya can train guide dogs.
• Use may to ask or give permission to do something.
  May I watch you train the dogs?

Sit/Set
• Use sit to mean "stay seated."
  Sit down during the class.
• Use set to mean "to put or place."
  Please set the leash in the corner.

Use can, may, sit, or set to complete each sentence.

1. May I watch the monkeys play?
2. This service dog can carry a large backpack.
3. You may sit here during the training film.
4. Hearing dogs can recall a person's name.
5. Watch the monkey set the plate on the table.
6. The monkeys may not climb on the furniture.
7. Did you teach these dogs to sit?
8. Some monkeys can brush people's hair and serve food.
9. This dog got the newspaper and set it on the porch.
10. May we take these service dogs out for a walk?

©2005 by Evan-Moor Corp. • EMC 4540 • Spell & Write — UNIT 12 — 117

Skills: Visual Sequencing; Recognizing Spelling Words

Word Search

Find and circle the spelling words. Words can go across, down, or diagonally.

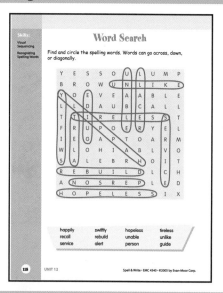

happily	swiftly	hopeless	tireless
recall	rebuild	unable	unlike
service	alert	person	guide

118 — UNIT 12 — Spell & Write • EMC 4540 • ©2005 by Evan-Moor Corp.

Skills: Writing a List

Helping Paws

You've read about the different ways animals help people. What other ways could animals help people? How could they help with sports or hobbies? Could they help at school? Write a list below. Be sure to write the kind of animal next to the task.

1. Responses will vary.
2.
3.
4.
5.
6.

Edit Your Work
○ I used correct spelling.
○ I used correct capitalization and punctuation.

120 — UNIT 12 — Spell & Write • EMC 4540 • ©2005 by Evan-Moor Corp.

Animal Friends

Skills: Writing a Poem

Do you know of or own a special animal? How does it help you or its owner? How is this animal a good friend to you or someone else? Write an acrostic poem about this animal. Begin each word, phrase, or sentence with a letter in the topic word.

F _____ Responses will vary.
R _____
I _____
E _____
N _____
D _____

©2005 by Evan-Moor Corp. • EMC 4540 • Spell & Write — UNIT 12 — 121

TEST YOUR SKILLS — **Animal Helpers** | **Spelling Test**

Find the correct answer. Fill in the circle.

1. Which sentence uses can or may correctly?
   ● Can this dog identify the sound of a siren?
   ○ This dog may identify many different sounds.
   ○ Some people in wheelchairs may not be able to move their arms or legs.

2. Which sentence uses sit or set correctly?
   ○ Binky can sit out food on the dinner table.
   ○ The monkey likes to set on your lap.
   ● Binky will sit in the chair until you call her.

3. Which word is spelled correctly?
   ● guide
   ○ gide
   ○ giude

4. Which word means "to warn or make someone aware of something"?
   ○ person
   ○ recall
   ● alert

5. Write the sentence correctly.
   sirvice animals hapily help people who want to rebuild their lives
   Service animals happily help people who want to rebuild their lives.

Spelling Test
Ask someone to test you on the spelling words.

1. _____
2. _____
3. _____
4. _____
5. _____
6. _____
7. _____
8. _____
9. _____
10. _____
11. _____
12. _____

122 — ASSESSMENT 12 — Spell & Write • EMC 4540 • ©2005 by Evan-Moor Corp.